Cycle Racing

Frank Westell and Ken Evans

Springfield Books Limited

© 1985 Frank Westell and Ken Evans

Published by Springfield Books Limited,
Norman Road, Denby Dale,
Huddersfield HD8 8TH, West Yorkshire,
England.

First edition 1985

Acknowledgements

The authors and publishers are grateful
to the following for permission to
include copright material:
Mike Dawson: pp. 22 (left), 42 (bottom),
70 (top left and right), 71, 72, 81, 105
(top), 106 (right), 125 (top), 127 and
136

Cover picture: The culmination of a
year's racing efforts for the world's best
road riders is the world road
championship. Here a Spanish rider
leads the field during the 1984 event at
Barcelona.
(Photo: Graham Watson)

Design: Douglas Martin
Photography: unless otherwise
acknowledged, all photos by Graham
Watson
Illustration: Anne Isseyegh
Typesetting and origination:
Paul Hicks Limited,
Burrington Way, Plymouth
Printed and bound in Italy by
Legatoria Editoriale Giovanni Olivotto,
Vicenza

ISBN 0-947655-01-8 (cased)
ISBN 0-947655-07-7 (paperback)

British Library Cataloguing in Publication Data

Westell, Frank
  Cycle racing.
  1. Bicycle racing
  I. Title   II. Evans, Ken
  796.6'2   GV1049

ISBN 0-947655-01-8

Contents

Set your body new limits

In cycle racing the super-champions are rare. To be a super-champion you need that combination of real natural talent plus the mental determination to make the most of that talent. You may be a super-champion in the making. But more likely you are one of thousands of cyclists who have real possibilities of being a champion of some sort, be it of your club, your country, or even the world.

We wrote this book to help you achieve your goal. For, make no mistake, everyone can improve through a systematic training programme. Your body thrives on being gradually set new limits.

There are riders in international jerseys who at the outset did not seem to have the right talents to succeed. But they have got the best out of themselves by the right mental approach, and by doing the right things. There are others at a high level who are supremely gifted physically, but never exploit those gifts to the full, and hence never reach their real potential – and that's sad.

Two of the super-champions of the eighties, in their natural habitat at the centre of media attention. Italy's Francesco Moser (right) staggered the world by shattering the hour record in 1984 when his career appeared to be on a downward path. Frenchman Bernard Hinault (below) dominated the Tour de France until 1983, when tendinitis forced him out.

You see the 'natural' in all walks of life. In cycling terms, he's the inexperienced rider who turns up for a club run and makes everyone suffer – who rides his first '10' and beats riders with years of experience. He quickly rises to be club champion, then division champion, and everyone tells him how good he is. But then the crunch comes: he meets tough opposition, and is likely to fall by the wayside, simply because he hasn't trained to capitalise on his talents. More often than not, he ends up being beaten by someone who is far less gifted, with less 'class', but who has been well trained and is determined to reach his personal limits of achievement.

A 'natural' at the beginning of his career. Sean Yates started as a time triallist, then quickly rose to the top as an amateur, and landed a contract with a continental professional team.

You're a 'natural' if you excelled at games in school. If you have a well-balanced body and a symmetrical musculature, and if your body chemistry allows you to take effort in your stride, then you have a start on so many others. If you're a 'natural', then look on your physical gifts as the key to a door marked 'success'. The ability to train hard and well will allow you to turn the door-handle and walk in.

But if, on the other hand, you don't recognise yourself as one of these potential winners, take comfort. The 'natural' often has life too easy, and can't face the mental load and the sheer drudgery of training. If he can, then he stands a chance of becoming a super-champion. If not, then you will just as likely end up beating him because of your superior determination and commitment to the task in hand – because you are prepared to give everything in pursuit of success, and not take the easy way out.

This book will tell you about racing, about training, about preparation and recovery, and about the techniques and skills and how to achieve them.

If you have a coach, then it will help you to understand his message better. If not, then it will do much of the work of a coach, and at the same time it will give you the stimulus of knowing what your training is about. You will be able to predict the effects of training, and this will give you greater satisfaction.

Cycle racing used to be unquestionably the province of the mainland Europeans – the French, Italians, Belgians and Dutch. And of course the heart of cycle racing is still there, with the immense public support and the fervour created by events like the Tour de France. But times are changing.

In 1974 a team of American amateurs came to Britain's Milk Race. Some people laughed at their inexperience then, but in the 1980s America has produced both world and Olympic champions.

You could tell even at that early stage that the Americans were going places, because of their thirst for knowledge. On that Milk Race they started out like every other ambitious bike-rider – by asking questions. But there the similarity ended, because the answers we

gave them produced more analytical questions, and then more still. Their quest for knowledge went beyond the immediate. We found one rider who had put the answers on tape for later study, and for passing on to other riders who hadn't quite made selection.

The Americans continue to pass on the knowledge and experience they have gained. Out of the 1976 Olympics team, Roger Young now trains a string of sprinters, while Jim Ochowicz is the manager of the 7-Eleven road team, and Ron Skarin is the national pursuit coach.

Between that first sortie into Europe and the present day, the USA has applied known scientific training principles to the experience it has gained in European racing. The scientific approach which had produced success in Olympic track and field events was used to do the same in cycling.

Now it's up to the rest of the world to adopt that new approach to cycle racing, and apply the latest scientific methods to our training. Otherwise, the Americas will go on to dominate world cycling – and deservedly. North America has taken the lead, and the rest of the Americas will follow in their wake. Unless the old traditions of cycle training, based on pre-war theories, are disregarded, the rest of the world will end up in their shadow, unable to benefit from the resurgence of interest in cycling.

Crowds at the finish of the Tour of Lombardy in 1983, with Irishman Sean Kelly winning the sprint. This is one of the European single-day classics which is the focus of attention for many thousands of fans.

The ideal racing cyclist

There is no such thing as an ideal build for a racing cyclist, but some extreme types of riders will have advantages or disadvantages depending on the type of event.

For example, the bulky type could be ideal for track sprinting but would be out of his depth in hilly road races. For some time trialling and pursuiting, a tall and lean rider will have the advantage of better streamlining. In road events a small rider will more easily take shelter and give his rivals little to shelter behind.

Perhaps the most useful physical attributes are long thighs and big feet, since these give increased leverage in the same way that long cranks are used to handle big gears.

The coaching role

What is coaching all about? Ultimately a coach gets the best from you, the rider, because of his past experience in the sport, and his ability to recognise your strengths and weaknesses, and then to work on them.

Coach and rider need to be on the same wavelength. They need to relate to one another and to have mutual respect. A cycling coach will usually have done some racing, but this isn't vital as long as he understands the needs of the sport and, above all, the principles of training. He should preferably be recognised by the cycling governing body.

It's your coach's job to advise you on a progressive training routine which will get you to the required standard. This doesn't mean blind acceptance of whatever he says. Nor does it mean you have to continually question his advice. There's plenty of room for you to ask your coach questions, and he should always be ready to give the answers. In this way you can get to understand the purpose of training and you'll be more likely to accept it. And later on, when you reach such a standard that you are away on racing trips without your usual coach, then you can work out how your training should be continuing

This means you are getting the best out of your coach, but not leaning on him so heavily that you are incapable of making your own intelligent training and racing decisions when he's not around.

You will find the word 'soigneur' turning up a lot, both in this book and, hopefully, during your racing career. A soigneur in cycling terms is a coach but a lot more besides. A coach primarily looks after a rider's training routines and development, whereas a soigneur gives advice on training, on build-up, and on basic health care as far as it affects cycling. But ideally your coach and your soigneur should be one and the same.

Successful coaches inspire enormous trust from a rider – and they should deserve that trust. Part of a soigneur's skill is in psychology – helping you overcome the mental problems posed by racing at a high level. Riders need to be able to talk over their problems with a trusted person who will not only sympathise but also analyse. A team meeting is rarely the place where you will want to give problems an airing. More frequently the racing and personal problems come out while you are relaxing on the massage plinth, or in a similar one-to-one situation. To a good coach or soigneur, feelings entrusted in this way should be like the secrets of the confessional. Any gossip or indiscretions threaten the bond with the rider.

It is vital for every cyclist to be able to pass on his feelings to his racing adviser. Without such

The coach needs feedback from his riders in order to give them the best advice. Russia's Kashirin gives after-race impressions following a Milk Race stage to his manager Viktor Kapitanov. Kapitanov has a distinguished racing pedigree, having won the road-race gold in the 1960 Olympics in Rome.

feedback, even the best of coaches can work only on a rider's physique, and never on his mind. Very often, just by voicing the problem to your soigneur, you will already start to see the solution. It is the problems unsolved, and worse, the problems unconsidered, which start to create stress. Even domestic stress can have adverse effects on training and racing.

So if you haven't a coach, then look for one. More than just a cycling expert who knows the sport and the theory of training, find someone who can communicate with you and doesn't just instruct you from a book. When you find him, you'll know him.

The road to success

You're looking for results, otherwise you wouldn't be reading this book. But how quickly will they come?

One of the ways to identify success as it comes is to know right from the outset where you are weak, and thus where you most need improvement. So take a good look at yourself, and tell yourself honestly where you are particularly bad. Are you strong but not fast? Are you fast but lacking in stamina? Are you strong and fast but a lousy tactician? Once you have identified your weaknesses, then concentrate on improving them. If you don't seem to have any particular strengths or weaknesses, then adopt a general training programme until they start to emerge.

Success won't come overnight, and any training plan must be a long-term one at first. Only when

you are well trained will you be adopting 'mini-plans' to peak for a given event perhaps only a few weeks ahead.

Training is tough and needs dedication. And that dedication disappears in most people if they cannot see some kind of progress – some short-term results. Happily, progressive training brings easily-identified improvements in a surprisingly short time – though you can't expect to go from a third-category licence to international status in a matter of weeks.

With youngsters the development pattern is different. Some youngsters who mature fast will note fast improvement beyond what their training might be expected to produce. Others, growing more slowly, might find themselves apparently slipping back in performance in relation to

Friendly smiles from Britons John Herety (left) and Paul Sherwen. Both burst upon the amateur scene after several years of working their way up through the ranks – getting their training right, and then committing themselves to a tough training programme. Both secured pro contracts abroad.

their friends or clubmates of a similar age. For instance, some 15-year-old boys are virtually men in their physique, while others are decidedly still boys. Consequently their results will be hard to compare. But in time there is a natural adjustment. By 18, comparisons are far easier.

So if you are in your teens and going through puberty, try to weigh up whether you're a good little 'un who still has plenty of growing to do, or whether you are growing faster than others of your age. In earlier years, late maturers have to face a period of being beaten by those who have simply developed more quickly. But the early maturers will have to face a 'levelling-off' period when the late maturers come back at them with a new challenge. If you are a youngster who has been quick to develop, and you find success comes easily as a result, then be prepared to redouble your training efforts at this 'levelling-off' time, or

when you graduate to senior status; otherwise you won't continue to progress.

Emotionally, the teenage years are a trying time; and one big pressure on youngsters is to be accepted and admired by their schoolmates or workmates. The tendency is to fall into doing what your friends do – and that is most unlikely to be cycle racing. Just remember that you are out for results, and you'll get them by concentrating on your training plan

instead of doing whatever seems more tempting at the time. For the most gifted and dedicated, cycle racing can provide a great career and international acclaim. At all levels it can be psychologically rewarding if you work hard.

Be prepared for setbacks. There are bound to be some, as these crash victims suddenly discovered during the Tour des Flandres in Belgium.

Even if all your friends are cyclists, you could end up following the crowd down the wrong path just because you don't want to set yourself apart. Remember that your training plan is for you, and not necessarily for anyone else.

Be prepared for setbacks. There are bound to be some all through your cycling career. Treat each setback as a challenge – a way of developing your character. Be determined to overcome setbacks, and that same determination will help you to be a winner.

Use your coach to help you through difficult times. At all levels it's common to find a rider approaching his coach feeling utterly downcast, convinced he's going nowhere. But a few minutes talking through the problem, hearing a fresh view of it, can result in new determination, the setbacks overcome, and a renewed approach to training and competition.

What are the ingredients of a champion? It's a question frequently asked, and the answer is complex. So many factors can be permutated to produce a winner, but the true champion has an abundance of the four S's:

Stamina
Strength
Speed
Skill

Some of these qualities are inborn, but all can be developed – and most champions have developed these factors rather than been born with them.

If you are starting out on the road to success, don't expect it to be a predictable journey. One of the intriguing aspects of training any sportsman or woman is that the results are only predictable to a degree. The more a rider contributes in meaningful training, the more benefits he should reap; but the mental aspect of training and sporting conflict can never be assessed at an early age. We have some superb methods – some simple, some highly scientific – of measuring sporting fitness. We can identify quite easily whether a rider's heart or muscle type is likely to make him a sprinter or a stage-race rider, a good climber or a fast finisher. But no one has yet developed a way of measuring a rider's determination to succeed. And determination can make up for some physical shortcomings.

On the other side of the coin, there are some riders who have all the physical attributes and seemingly also the mental attributes of being a champion: but they simply cannot perform when subjected to the greater stress of the Olympics, World Championships or Commonwealth Games.

So let's go on down the road towards your personal goal, and attempt to discover, through good technique and good training, how best you can achieve it – or even surpass it.

However a rider starts his career, he may achieve his final glory in an entirely different field. Belgium's Patrick Sercu (centre) was a world champion sprinter. Dutchman Rene Pijnen (nearest camera) was a good amateur and pro roadman. But together they made a new reputation for themselves in a virtually unbeatable six-day racing team.

2 Road racing

The world-wide appeal

Road racing is the most widespread form of cycle racing in world terms, and certainly draws the most attention from the public, through the Tour de France, the big single-day classics of Europe, and Britain's own Milk Race.

Road racing covers single-day road races and stage races. The latter are events comprising two or more road races, sometimes with a time trial thrown in: the overall winner is the rider with the shortest total time for all the stages — he need not win any of them.

To be an effective road-racing cyclist, you must be able to time-trial, to ride in a tightly-packed bunch, to climb and descend hills, and to finish the race like a trackman; on rough courses you must have the agility of a cyclo-cross rider! In short, the top roadman should be able to shine in time trialling and track racing, but it doesn't necessarily work the opposite way.

The essence of road racing is to combine the ability to ride fast with the ability to make efforts only when necessary, and to reach the line first by a combination of fitness and tactics.

So often you hear at the end of a race that the winner 'didn't do a tap', and that someone else was the man of the race. Unfortunately, the record books list only winners, and not 'men of the race'. Remember, the final argument is to win!

However, if you admire the 'moral victor' over the man who beats him without 'doing a tap', you can be

Road racing demands a multitude of skills: short-circuit criteriums need speed; hilly road races need strength and stamina; some events require the talents of a cyclo-cross rider. Pictured here are a Kelloggs criterium at Bristol in 1983 (with Sean Yates in the lead), the 1983 Milk Race tackling Farndale Moor, and the cobbles of the 1984 Paris–Roubaix.

comforted by the knowledge that the winner will eventually get his just deserts. For every tough race is first-class training, and if you have ridden hard and lost, you may have gained more in fitness than the actual winner.

The main difference between road racing and time trialling is that in road racing the rider uses the presence of others to make riding easier or to go faster. In bunched racing, the art of slipstreaming — 'sitting in' — is vital to conserving energy. This means that a bunch of riders sharing the pace can go faster than one rider of similar ability. But the bigger the bunch and the less determined the riders in it, the more chance a lone breakaway rider has of reaching the finishing-line ahead.

Road racing is not just riding fast: it is making a series of tactical judgements, often in a split second. Do you chase this rider who has broken away, or will he 'die'? Do you let someone else chase him? Should you bother working in this breakaway once you've caught it, or do the riders look like they can't sustain the break to the finish? Do you go for a long sprint or a short one? Which side of the road? Are you as strong as you think? Is the other man as weak as he looks — or says?

No one has ever made all the right decisions in road racing; but with every decision you make, you broaden your experience.

Classic road-racing machines from the Raleigh stable in Nottingham: with alloy components, a frame of aircraft-grade alloy steel tubing, and medium-weight wheels with small-flange hubs.

The road-racing bike

The classic road-racing machine has developed over the years, from the very early days of the century when the 'giants of the road' used single-geared heavyweights with tyres which would be scorned by today's cyclo-cross riders. The advent of the derailleur gear – giving a choice of three different gear ratios, and eventually the typical twelve of today – has changed the whole character of road racing. The perfection of techniques for forging aluminium alloy has brought yet more changes.

Today's road machine is a joy to behold – and even a joy to assemble, such is the precision of current components.

This book is not a technical tome or a repair manual, and today's cycling magazines contain much good advice on choice of components; so we'll content ourselves here with a broad description of the types of parts and accessories which make up the machine.

The frame

The frame is made of seamless lightweight-alloy steel tubing, such as Reynolds 531 or 753, Columbus, Ishiwata or Vitus. Occasionally you will also find a frame of aluminium alloy, which is light but not as rigid; thus some of the pedalling energy is soaked up by the tubes, as they deflect more than a steel tube.

The tubes are held together by lugs: thin metal jointing pieces which vary in styling. They function quite simply as sleeves, joining the tubes together with the help of a thin layer of molten brass or silver solder.

The fit of the tubes, and the craft of the man brazing them together, decides how 'good' the frame will be. Two frames of equal dimensions and materials can differ in their handling because the jointing has not been carried out equally well; hence the tubes in an inferior machine can move more in relation to each other, with a consequent loss of pedalling energy.

Frame design is important, and will vary according to the machine's ultimate use. Most off-the-peg frames are good compromises, and can be used to good effect by judicious adjustment of the saddle and handlebar positions. But this didn't stop riders like the great Belgian, Eddy Merckx, who in the Tour de France took several different bicycles with him for different types of stages. The most obvious 'special' frame will be for time trialling, where lightness is of paramount importance. But Merckx would have other bikes with frames specially designed for circuit races, mountain stages, and those ridden over cobbles.

A frame's handling will change with the length of the tubes involved, and the angles between them. For example, the more upright the head tube, the more volatile is the steering. However, a very shallow head-tube angle will

(bent) affects the handling. Track bikes have virtually straight forks because they do not need to be steered around tight corners. But if ridden on a rough road, straight forks will shake the headset loose and eventually have a similar effect on the rider!

So the typical road machine has fairly steep head and seat angles (73 degrees being typical), gently raked forks, and chain stays which are only just long enough for the rear wheel to be removed without having to deflate the tyre. It is designed with the bottom bracket high enough so that the rider can pedal through many corners without grounding the inside pedal.

The wheels

The wheels should be light enough for the job in hand, and will vary in spoking accordingly. It is important to ride the lightest wheels consistent with the type of event, because weight saved on revolving components (wheels, tyres, cranks, pedals) is worth more than weight saved on relatively static components such as handlebars or saddle.

Bearing in mind that the average road race will not be on billiard-table surfaces, the typical choice will be a 22mm-wide rim, with 36 spokes and small-flange hubs (quick-release, of course). This gives a wheel which will accept all but the narrowest tubulars, and which will happily take the minor shocks of rough road surfaces because of the longer spokes used with small-flange hubs.

On smooth-road events such as time trials, large-flange hubs and

Frenchman Bernard Hinault uses a special time-trial bike. The lightweight tubing is oval instead of round, the brake cables are concealed, and the machine is built for speed over a short distance.

produce a bike which steers well but gives a less responsive ride. A longer wheelbase, with a shallow head angle and long chain stays, produces a comfortable machine but one which soaks up a lot of effort.

Even the way the forks are raked

fewer spokes might be recommended.

Lighter riders or smooth pedallers might get away with a 32-spoked wheel, at least on the front wheel; but the weight saved is negligible.

In really vital events where the rider wants to maximise his chances and has recourse to plenty of spare wheels, 28-spoked wheels could be used for that extra boost. But it's risky.

It is important that wheels should be kept in good condition. Much of road racing depends on good bike-handling and instant responses, and this can be compromised every time you brake if your rim is slightly buckled and you get a juddering effect on the steering. Wheels which cannot be properly trued should be relegated to the training equipment store.

The tyres

Choice of tyres will again depend on the course and on the road surface. Generally speaking, cotton tubulars are the standard choice for road racing, with silk tyres for special events. Silk tubulars give extra 'zip'; but unless their walls are latex-coated they should not be used in the rain, because they don't react well to getting wet, and will lose the 'zippy' feel that characterises silk tyres.

If you can afford it, go for latex-tubed tubulars. They have slightly better puncture resistance and give a more responsive ride than a butyl-tubed model with the same weight. Average road-racing tyres will weigh around 250 grams (8½ ounces), and will have a mixed tread to give both speed and grip on the corners. Smooth-band or ribbed tubulars are best avoided for road racing.

Keep your tyres in good condition, always partially inflated on a rim when not in use. Inspect them after every race for cuts in the tread or bulges. Tread cuts can sometimes be tackled with tread-stopping compound, but if in doubt relegate the offending tyre to the training stock or the dustbin.

For your 'spare' use a good tyre which has been mounted on a rim. It should first be folded in half either side of the valve, then rolled up tightly with the tread always on the outside of the bend. Finally, wrap the entire tubular in a waterproof covering such as PVC or polythene, and strap it underneath the saddle. Spare tyres do fit in a bottle-cage, but then they can often get chafed and damaged. Don't use a new tyre as a spare, because it will be hard to fit if a quick change is needed, and will not have any rim cement on the base tape.

The transmission

Road-racing machines always have double chainsets of light alloy, with chainwheels that can be easily changed to give a different set of gear ratios as required.

Cranks are typically 170mm long; but younger riders or particularly nimble pedallers may prefer to go as low as 165mm, while big-gear pushers and more powerful riders will move up the scale to 172.5 or 175mm for greater leverage. If in doubt, stick with 170mm, which is a happy medium.

Pedals are a matter of choice, but bear in mind that their purpose is to support the foot. If you've an extra-wide foot, make sure the pedal is wide too.

Choice of toe-clip length is very important. Between them, the toe-clip, strap and shoe-plate on the sole of your shoe ensure that you get the best out of your pedalling power.

The shoe-plate actually positions the foot by slotting into the pedal, and should be located so that the broadest part of the foot is immediately above the pedal axle. This much established, the toe-clip should be long enough to leave just a chink of daylight between the toe of the shoe and the front of the toe-clip. There should not be any contact.

In practice, a short toe-clip is best for riders who take a size 40 shoe (British size 6) or less, a medium one for up to about size 42 (or 8), and long thereafter. But don't take this as a hard and fast rule: get your foot placed correctly, and choose the toe-clip length accordingly.

Good toe-straps are important, because they need to hold firm when the foot is pulling up against the clip on the pedalling upstroke – frequently with violent acceleration. Any slippage of the buckle here may cause your foot to fly out of the clip, with disastrous results.

The gearing

Gearing will obviously vary according to the terrain of the event; but the modern derailleur copes so well that riders nowadays tend to change their gearing set-up very little during the season, unless they suddenly have to tackle a very hilly event.

The idea is to have two ranges of gearing: one on the small, inside chainring for climbing, and the other on the outside ring for fast work. Thus, if you are suddenly

Italy's Francesco Moser demonstrates why road racing bikes have to be sturdy: the rake of the forks helps to soak up the buffeting of the cobbled road; the rubber hoods on the brake levers offer some form of cushioning to the hands; and the toe-clip takes much of the stress when the foot is pulling the pedal upwards. Note the clear gap between the front of his left shoe and the metal of the toe-clip.

confronted with a hill, you can drop easily on to the bottom ring and immediately change down considerably without complication.

In effect, this is achieved with two fairly widely spaced chainrings – say 42 and 53 – and a six-speed freewheel block which is either one-tooth 'straight through' 13–18, or possibly 13–21 in averagely hilly country. Thus your two ranges on the 13–18 are 87.2, 81.0, 75.6, 70.9, 66.7 and 63.0 (on the 42 ring), and 110.0, 102.2, 95.4, 89.4, 84.1 and 79.5 (on the 53 ring). In practice you would not use the 42 x 13 and the 53 x 18, because you would not want such extreme deflection of the chain from a theoretical straight line.

Each one-tooth change on the freewheel gives a very subtle gear difference; but if, for instance, you meet a sudden hill when motoring fast on 53 x 15, you can quickly change down 20 inches by dropping on to the small ring. To make effective use of this big gear-change in both directions, your front changer must be precisely adjusted, so that you can push the lever right forward or pull it right back with absolute confidence.

The 42/53 rings and the 13–18 and 13–21 blocks are for top-line riders, of course. Juniors on the road are restricted to 86.4, and schoolboys in circuit events to 76.2; so a different range needs to be adopted accordingly, but using the same principle. A complete gear table can be found in the appendices.

When picking freewheel blocks, bear in mind that they are usually found in five-, six- or seven-speed versions. The seven-speed blocks have narrow spacing between the sprockets to fit in the width of a standard six-speed. There are also narrow six-speeds which fit in the width of a standard five. Most popular these days are the narrow and standard six-speeds.

Once again, it is vital that your rear derailleur operates positively. This means you must buy a good mechanism in the first place, and then clean it regularly to make sure that the action of the pivots is not impaired by dirt and grit.

The brakes

The brakes too are evidently important, since their good operation allows you to corner with confidence, knowing that you can exactly time your application and release of your brakes.

In the fifties, the use of centre-pull brakes by top roadmen was almost universal; but fashion has swung back to the use of short-stirrup side-pulls, which are more rigid than centre pulls and, if properly adjusted, just as powerful in operation.

Brake levers should carry rubber hoods for cushioning when, as frequently happens even in racing, you are using the brake hoods as a hand rest. Angle the brake levers so that a) they are comfortable and b) you can easily reach them when you are riding on the drops.

It is also important to adjust the brakes so that they come into effect quite rapidly. If you need to squeeze the levers almost back to the handlebars before maximum braking is achieved, then they are wrongly adjusted.

Handlebars and saddle

Handlebar shape is a matter of personal preference, but the chosen bar should give you three comfortable riding positions: on the drops, on the brake-lever hoods, and on the tops either side of the handlebar-stem clamp.

Handlebar width is not a matter of preference: it should be suited to your build. The bars should be just wide enough so that your outstretched arms do not in any way constrict your lung expansion. Usually this width is 40cm (measured from the centre of the handlebar tube at each side); but younger riders and women may prefer 38cm, and broader riders 42cm or very occasionally 44cm.

The other extremity is the saddle, which must support a great proportion of the body weight and therefore needs to be slightly padded. Traditionally, leather saddles were always used, because the leather moulded itself to the rider's anatomy during a suitable 'breaking-in' period; hence a rider would transfer his treasured and personalised saddle from bike to bike. With the advent of plastic saddles – which needed no breaking in and were basically unharmed by bad weather – leather saddles suddenly became old-fashioned. Modern saddles combine the best of both worlds, with a nylon or plastic base covered by foam padding and then topped off by a covering of smooth or suede leather.

Position for road racing

When the pedal is at its lowest point, the leg is not quite straight, as Daniel Gisiger of Switzerland demonstrates.

The purpose of a good body position is to ensure maximum comfort and efficiency from the point of view of both pedalling and aerodynamics.

Correctly positioned, the rider can use his legs to best advantage. By bracing back and shoulders, he can if necessary increase leg-thrust by the pull of his arms on the bars. To understand the principle, think of how you pull on a wellington boot: you first insert the foot with the leg bent, then start to straighten the leg while pulling the boot towards you, against the force of the straightening leg. In this way your arm-pull increases the effect of your leg-thrust, and you can bring even more force to bear by starting with a slightly bent back and straightening that at the same time.

There are three points of contact between the body and the bike: the saddle, the pedals and the handlebars. Of these, the first ones to get right are at the saddle and the pedals. These are determined by the position of your saddle, not only in height but in relation to the pedals when the main pedal-thrust is applied. The idea is to set your saddle so that the pelvis does not need to roll from side to side as you pedal, and so that the leg is not quite fully extended at the bottom of the pedal stroke.

To find this position (and often a friend can help in this), you should mount your bike wearing your racing shoes, and prop yourself upright. Now put your heels on the pedals and start to pedal backwards. If you are sliding from side to side on the saddle to reach the lower pedal, then gradually lower your saddle just to the point where that is no longer necessary. You will then find that your leg is at its fullest natural extension without having to stretch at all.

Now your saddle height is correct, but we are not finished with your saddle adjustment yet. Mount the bike again, this time with your feet in the toe-clips. Set the cranks horizontally – that is, at a quarter to three. Now call in your friendly observer and get him to judge, with a weighted line if necessary, the relative positions of your forward knee and the pedal axle. If you are correctly positioned, the knee cap should be vertically above the pedal axle.

When you adjust your saddle forward or backward to achieve this, remember that this will also produce a slight decrease or increase in the distance from pedal to saddle; so you may need to readjust your saddle height accordingly until both measurements are correct.

Finally, make sure that your saddle top is horizontal; this will avoid your crutch being numbed if you slide forwards or backwards on the saddle.

To determine whether your handlebar position is right, sit on the saddle with your hands holding the

This is Ireland's Sean Kelly as seen from behind. Note the bend in the leg when the crank is at its lowest, and the way the upper knee comes just inside the flexed elbow. The shoe-plate on the left-hand pedal can be clearly seen.

With cranks horizontal, the front of the knee should be over the pedal axle. Bernard Hinault demonstrates this. Note also the way he drags up on the rising pedal.

bars on the drops, in the normal racing position. Now set your forward crank parallel to the down tube. In this position, with your arms very slightly bent, the knee should just be able to graze the inside of the elbow. You can achieve this by changing your stem length or possibly your handlebar shape.

Finally, you may need to rotate your handlebars slightly to make sure that, when you ride 'on the drops', your wrist is naturally straight and in line with your forearm.

This basic position is automatically modified according to circumstances. When the going is really hard, the arms come more into play and you slide forward on the saddle – hence the phrase 'on the rivet'.

Conversely, when you are using a small gear, either for pedalling easily or for twiddling your way up a climb, you will aim for more suppleness in your pedalling. You hold the tops of the bars and naturally slide back on the saddle.

This position will enable you to pedal naturally, using your ankle joint to raise or drop the heel at various points on the pedal-stroke. Near the top of the stroke the heel drops slightly to push forward when the cranks are vertical; then, as the pedal is thrust downwards, the foot

goes toe-down; at the bottom, the toe claws the pedal round, while the foot becomes horizontal and then goes heel-down towards the end of the up-stroke. If you pedal toe-down for the whole of the revolution you are a) probably sitting too high and b) not making use of the potentially powerful shin muscles to aid your pedalling power.

You can make very minor adjustments as the need arises. For very long events you might drop your saddle fractionally and raise your handlebars accordingly; but normally your basic position should not need to be altered.

Clothing

When you are road racing you need to be comfortable and warm, and aerodynamically clothed without being constricted. You need to be able to carry food and drink in an easily-accessible position, and you must be reasonably protected against crash damage. All this adds up to a smart and functional outfit which has varied little over the years. Any changes due to advances in fabric technology have been basically cosmetic.

Undervest

You should always wear a cotton or wool-based short-sleeved vest, with plenty of length to cover the lower back when you are bent over. This serves two purposes: firstly to soak up sweat so it does not feel clammy next to the skin, secondly to give some protection against abrasions and lacerations if you crash. The top-layer jersey slides against the undervest instead of the skin, and grazes are reduced as a result.

Shorts

Never wear anything underneath racing shorts, which should be cut so that they are close-fitting but still comfortable. They should be lined on the crutch with chamois leather, which is sewn into the shorts with seams that do not rub against the sensitive perineum – the area which is actually in contact with the saddle and thus most liable to chafing. The chamois should be lubricated for

A moment of relaxation, giving a good view of the classic road-racing clothing: woollen jersey, cotton cap, close-fitting shorts extending well down the thigh, white ankle socks and leather cycling shoes. The rider nearest camera wears arm-warmers.

each major outing with special softening grease, usually lanolin-based and sometimes containing antiseptic. There are several purpose-made preparations on the market.

The shorts should not be tight at the waist, as this might restrict circulation to the lower limbs. Instead, they can either be held up by lightweight braces, or else have integral braces of their own, in which case they are known as 'bib shorts'.

Shorts used always to be made of wool-based materials, and many experienced riders still insist on shorts with a majority of wool in the

material. Wool-based shorts are comfortable, warm and absorbent. However, acrylic shorts are easier to wash and dry, and are cheaper. 'Skinshorts' are a more recent development. They are made of yarn containing some form of elastomeric material, the most well-known type being Lycra. This is light to wear and stretchy, so a good aerodynamic fit is assured. However, skinshorts are not warm, and could be a positive drawback in early-season events.

Whichever type of shorts material you choose, make sure of a good fit at the crutch, and minimise the danger of saddle soreness and consequent infections by washing your shorts frequently and thoroughly. During a stage race you should have a clean pair for each stage, so you will need several pairs altogether. Make sure the shorts are washed in soap flakes, well rinsed, and then dried gradually, gently stretching out the chamois insert as it dries. If you dry it quickly and artificially, it will turn into an efficient piece of sandpaper.

Jersey

Racing jerseys for road racing usually have three pockets at the rear just below waist level. These are for carrying food, and sometimes a spare tyre or a bottle if your bike doesn't have a bottle cage (which it should!). The jersey can be made of wool, wool/acrylic or a variety of man-made fibres. It should be close-fitting, and stay that way, without being constricting. It should also be long enough to cover the lower back even when you are fully bent forward.

Again, wool-based jerseys are naturally best, although they need more careful washing. They retain body heat better, making them warmer in cold weather, without being particularly hot in very warm weather. There are jerseys made of Lycra-based material, but they are only suitable for short events and offer no appreciable warmth. They are most frequently found as combination 'skinsuits' – shorts and jersey combined – and are very popular with track riders and time triallists.

Jerseys can have long or short sleeves depending on the weather. A useful accessory is a pair of detachable sleeves – 'arm-warmers' – which can be donned for the start of a cold event and transferred to a rear pocket if you warm up sufficiently. Leg-warmers exist, too, but it's difficult to take them off in the middle of a race without presenting your rivals with a golden opportunity to give you the slip!

Footwear

Ankle socks (white is the rule) are essential for healthy feet. Riding without socks is just inviting chafing, irritation and infection. However, the socks should not be so thick at the sole that you lose the 'feel' of your shoes, and should preferably be made of wool or cotton mixture. Acrylics are easy to wash but soon get baggy. Nylon socks usually make the feet sweat too much, and are consequently not recommended for anything except the shortest events.

Wear your preferred ankle socks when trying on your racing shoes for the first time. Here, for once, you can allow yourself the luxury of buying something which is tight, at least at the sides, because new leather stretches to accommodate itself to the foot:

No real substitute for leather uppers has been found. Even those rather clever shoes with nylon-mesh uppers have extensive leather supporting bars. Leather soles are preferred too, because then the feet can breathe easily. However, leather substitutes or rubber compounds are possible for riders on a limited budget.

Many good racing shoes have shoe-plates already fitted. If not, you should fit separate shoe-plates of metal or nylon. Fitting shoe-plates is a painstaking business, and extremely important. Shoe-plates have a deep slot which engages the rear cage-plate of the pedal, and allows you to push forwards and pull backwards on the pedal as well as pushing down. The slot is never a tight fit, so some latitude is allowed here; but the positioning of the plates should follow the position naturally adopted by the unrestricted shod foot in the toe-clip.

Fitting shoe-plates is done only after a good ride in the shoes – long enough to allow the pedal cage-plates to leave an impression on the sole. Using a soft pencil, extend the rear pedal mark on either side so that it covers the width of the shoe. Now position the shoe-plate so that the slot falls parallel to the pencil line but just an eighth of an inch in front of it. This ensures that your shoe, when engaged in the shoe-plate, will not rub against the front of the toe-clip.

Many shoes have shoe-plates already fitted; but this is only a good idea if the plates can also be adjusted to get perfect placement, not only forwards and backwards, but also at the correct angle. No two people hold their legs at the same angle below the knee, hence the need for individual adjustment.

Headgear

In most countries you must wear a crash-hat when road racing. There are many types of head protection, from the downright flimsy to the preposterously heavy. Most of them at least cut down the risk of head injuries, especially abrasive ones.

An extra pound or so spent on a better crash hat is always worth it. Look for firm padding on the protective bars, protective padding behind the ears, and a comfortable strap which is absolutely secure. Make sure that the hat fits well, and doesn't tip back easily to leave your temple unprotected.

In hot or rainy weather a cotton cap affords extra protection from the weather, and can be worn under or over the crash-hat according to preference. The cap also soaks up sweat and rain and stops it running into your eyes.

Mitts

In even the most minor crashes, you can sustain some nasty scars on the palms of your hands, since the natural instinct when falling is to stretch out your arms for protection. So *always* wear well-fitting track mitts with leather or chamois palms. The backs can be of leather, crochet or Lycra but this is a matter of personal preference. A good padded palm is a must for protection, and it also stops your

Contrasts in clothing at a British criterium. Sid Barras (centre) has chosen a skinsuit, since no pockets will be needed for this short event; while Francesco Moser (right) has gone for a traditional road-racing jersey, with plenty of length at the back. Barras wears a typical lightweight road-racing crash helmet without a cap, while Phil Anderson (left) wears his helmet beneath his cap.

Racing in the rain. The cotton cap is here keeping the rain out of Sean Yates' eyes, while a nylon racing cape keeps off the worst of the weather. It will be discarded later, when the weather or the pace hots up.

hands aching from many miles of riding over rough surfaces. The fit should be very snug.

Cape

In rainy weather, a racing cape is sometimes worthwhile. This is a jacket which opens all the way down the front; it is cut like a voluminous track top and made of nylon. Racing capes become extremely hot with use, and should therefore only be used in very cold rainy weather, or in the early part of a long event when the speed is not expected to be high. Once the weather or the pace hots up, it can quickly be discarded or bundled up into a jersey pocket.

Techniques and tactics

You can practise road-racing techniques when out riding for pleasure, alone or in a group. For much of the skill in bunched racing is simply a matter of dealing effectively with the problems posed by terrain. The climbs and descents, the corners, the rough roads, are the ever-present adversaries which must be continually overcome, all the time you are tackling the human rivals alongside you in the race.

You must work to overcome the problems of the course by training until you react automatically to the course, leaving you free to devote your energies to the *real* rivals. This means taking every opportunity to perfect your technique: every time you take a corner; every time you climb or descend a hill, or cross a stretch of rough road.

Cornering

Despite the fact that only a few square centimetres of rubber is its tenuous contact with the road surface, the road-racing bicycle is remarkably stable at speed, providing you don't try to dissuade it too much from a straight line. Thus the key to cornering fast and safely is to eliminate as much of the corner as you can and to choose a riding line which is as near a straight line as possible.

The more you turn the handlebars, the more your front wheel, acting under gyroscopic forces, tries to turn them back again. It likes being ridden in a straight line. So the worst way of cornering is to ride straight up the road, brake hard at the last moment, wrench the bars round, and hug the inside of the bend all the way. Do it this way, and you will lose lengths on every corner – lengths which, as you kick your bike into speed again from a very low cornering velocity, are hard to get back.

The fastest way through a corner is not necessarily the shortest way. If you corner too tightly, you will lose time fighting the bike's tendency to drift outwards. Far better to ease the bike through the corner by persuading it that the corner hardly exists.

Let's take a 90-degree left-hand bend as an example. The correct technique is to move out to the right as you approach the bend: either to the crown of the road if you are racing in normal conditions, or even further to the right on closed roads. Then steer gently, leaning the bike rather than turning the bars, towards the point of the bend, aiming almost to clip the kerb at the apex of the corner, providing the road surface at this point is uncomplicated by drainholes,

Cornering technique in a bunch. Note that the lead rider, Dudley Hayton, has swept across the road to take the corner at its apex, leaning over with the bike otherwise following a straight line. He is not braking at all, and is pedalling through the bend. Unusually, his inner leg is down (contrast with the second rider's technique), but this is because he is pedalling and knows he will not touch the road surface even at the pedal's lowest point. Succeeding riders demonstrate the line through the corner.

degree of braking; but try to complete your braking on the entry to the bend, so that you are fully under control as you take the corner itself, and are better able to accelerate again. On downhill hairpin bends, you may actually have to shift your bodyweight across to the inside of the bike to get round – not quite like a yachtsman in a high wind, but following a similar principle.

Road racing itself can teach you a lot, especially if you follow an experienced rider through corners. At first you may back off because you lack the confidence; but later you will be content to follow a faster and more experienced rider through, and pick up his technique by imitation.

Corners are an opportunity to wreak havoc on rivals. If you lead into a corner you are in the controlling position. Those behind you can only react to what you do. Ease off unexpectedly and your rivals will be grabbing at the brakes, only to find you accelerating away immediately. Sprint out of a corner and the delay in acceleration is magnified as it passes down the line, giving the riders at the end of the string a tough task to stay in contact.

This whiplash effect on riders following a leader – the further back in the string, the worse the effect is – means that the exits from corners are prime places to attack your rivals. You won't necessarily get clear, but at least your effort will wear them down and there isn't anything they can do about it.

If you are one of the riders following the leader, then your obvious tactic is to make sure you're in front for the next corner and try to turn the tables. But there

Italy's Saronni takes a corner alone. Note that the handlebars are hardly turned. Instead, the rider is leaning his body and the bike to effect the manoeuvre. Eyes are firmly fixed in the direction of eventual travel.

manholes, gravel or potholes. Then let the bike drift out towards the middle of the road again as it wants, subject to any traffic hazard; and gradually correct your course as the road straightens out.

Depending on your bike, your nerve and the camber of the road, you may be able to pedal all the way. At worst, you will have to stop pedalling momentarily, with your inside knee up and pointed slightly outwards.

Hopefully you won't even have had to brake, which spares you the extra disrupting forces caused by making the bike decelerate faster than it likes. Acceleration out of the corner is smooth and fully under control.

Even tighter bends may need a

Corners can offer an opportunity to wreak havoc on rivals. Sprint out of them and you compel those behind you to an ever-increasing effort to stay in touch.

is another way of using a corner to your advantage. This is to swing wider on the approach to the corner and steer tighter. As the rider in front starts to drift out on the exit, you are already sprinting along a line to take yourself inside him, launching an attack.

When you are training in a group, try this scenario so you can perfect it.

Hill climbing

Each rider has his own way of tackling hills, which will make use of his particular skills and physical gifts.

On the long mountain passes of the Tour de France, the Luxembourger Charly Gaul would sit back on his saddle, body upright, hands holding the tops of the bars, and concentrating on twiddling a very low gear. They called him the 'Angel of the Mountains', but he gave the others a devil of a time. One of his rivals was Gastone Nencini of Italy, who like Gaul also became a Tour de France winner. Nencini wasn't a gifted climber, but he had amazing powers of recuperation after anaerobic efforts. His technique on mountain passes was to launch himself into a devastating uphill sprint, ease to cruising pace, let his rivals catch him up, then launch another sprint, repeating the tactic until he broke them.

His talent was a rare one indeed, since generally speaking the long climbs are best tackled by settling into a good working rhythm and not deviating from it unnecessarily.

Experienced riders like Britain's Barry Hoban would know their limitations on the long climbs. If the super-climbers were on the rampage, Hoban – and many others like him – would not be tempted to hang grimly on to the leaders. Instead, he would settle into a pace he could maintain to the summit, then launch himself into a chasing effort on the descent and the flat roads which followed.

Of course, this patient technique is of little use on the short climbs. Hills are the classic 'killing ground' for a rider who aims to destroy a field of rivals. If you lose contact, you will have to make uneconomic efforts to get back afterwards. So it's important to stay in touch if you can.

If you know a climb, you can better judge how to tackle it. Some hills are tackled by a sprinter's effor – out of the saddle all the way until over the summit. Others are simply too long for that, and should be tackled mostly in the saddle.

Riding out of the saddle – or 'honking' as it is sometimes called – isn't an efficient way of climbing a hill, but it is effective in terms of speed. The technique is to lift your body off the saddle and 'dance' on the pedals, swinging the bike to and fro between your thighs but basically keeping the body going in a straight line. In this way you are in effect pulling up on the handlebars on the same side as the descending pedal, using the power of your shoulders to augment the strength of your thighs in pushing the pedal down. It's the same principle that you use when pulling on your wellingtons.

Making more use of your

'Honking' – the fast way of getting up a hill using the strength of the shoulders to augment that of the legs. This is Dutchman Joop Zoetemelk. Note that the body stays almost vertical, while the bike sways from side to side between the rider's thighs as he dances on the pedals.

shoulders and arms in this way increases your power output, so you will soon feel the familiar ache in your thighs as you go into oxygen debt. You start to gasp; your system is no longer efficiently getting rid of the toxins produced by effort, and there is a painful build-up of acid in the muscles. This is why you won't

be honking for very long if you are really making an effort. Soon you will be forced to sit back on the saddle and climb at a slower rate. So save the honking for times when you are under pressure or hoping to put others under pressure.

A more efficient way to tackle climbs is to sit well back in the saddle, take a good grip on the tops of the handlebars and concentrate on turning the pedals rhythmically. Gear too high and you will have trouble getting the pedals past 'top dead centre' when the cranks are vertical. As you start the forward and downward push on the pedals, pull back on the bars to increase the power you are applying. Concentrate on pulling up on the pedals as well as pushing down. Make sure you are breathing deeply and rhythmically – in time with the pedals if this is comfortable.

Climbing technique on a long climb. Hands grip the tops of the bars; rider John Herety is firmly in the saddle and turning a low gear.

When tackling long climbs in a working group, try to avoid easing back too much when you have finished your turn in front. Keep changes in pace to a minimum, and you will avoid developing 'dead legs'.

Hills are a natural place to attack. The speed is slower than on the flat, and therefore the 'slipstreaming effect' is minimised: a rider saves less energy by placing himself right behind you than he does on flat roads. So you can even attack from the leading position (a mistake in other circumstances), and open a gap if you are strong enough.

Working on a climb. The left-hand rider is falling back to take a breather, but is still out of the saddle to make sure he does not lose too much speed.

One of the better moments to attack is across the top of a climb. Riders who have reacted to attacks on a climb, or who are simply having trouble with the gradient, tend to measure their effort to the top, knowing life will be easier on the descent. With a few metres to go to the top, the last thing they want to do is to produce a big effort to react to an attack. Launching an

Towards the top of a climb, no one looks keen on making an attack. For the strong man, now could be the moment to do just that.

offensive move when a climb is all but over is tantamount to kicking a man when he's down. But in road racing you must always look to attack when your adversaries are most likely to be unwilling to react quickly. A steep climb, easing just before the top, and a good section of flat before the ensuing descent – that's an ideal combination of conditions to make your move if you can. Attacking this way is no great surprise move – every experienced rider expects it – but nevertheless, they still don't want to react and would prefer if someone else did the chasing. With everyone leaving the pursuit to everyone else, you can see what happens: nobody chases, and you have opened a gap in no time.

What happens if you're bad on hills? Well, recognise the fact, and cut your losses by making sure you're in the best position when approaching a climb. Sit well up in the bunch or group, and then when the pressure goes on you can slip gradually back in the field and hopefully still be in the bunch – maybe among the

tail-enders – when the climb is over. If you start a climb at the back, then the pressure will shoot you quickly and irrevocably out at the back. If there is one good climber in your group, then it doesn't hurt to place yourself ahead of him. As you start to slow up, he finds he is going slower than he'd like, and has to make an unwelcome effort to kick round you and move up again. All the time you are riding at *your* pace, and hopefully staying in contact.

Gear selection is important. Change down before you have to; keep the gears on the low side, and you can always react by speeding up your pedalling rate. Ride too high a gear, and you aren't flexible enough to react. Finally, be aware of changes in gradient, and change gear accordingly. And vary your line according to gradient, too. On tight uphill bends, don't hug the shortest inside line if the actual gradient steepens – as it usually does.

Descending

If you are a lousy climber, then you might get some encouragement from the fact that the world's best climbers are usually terrible descenders. So if you trail over the top of an Alp several minutes down, you have the chance to make it up again if you're good at going downhill. Bad climbers should work at descending well.

Descending is a mixture of nerve and technique. The nerve might be there to begin with, and is either improved or worsened by experience. Technique is a matter of realising what factors affect a descending rider.

When you are tackling a long descent, you are buffeted by a

greater airstream than when riding fast on the flat. The wind resistance is felt on downhill straights, and especially on corners, since your very speed around a downhill bend can create problems you wouldn't experience were the bend on the flat.

To get the best from a descent, get as near as you can to the downhill skier's egg position: crouch over the bars, with your shoulders and elbows tucked in, cranks at a quarter to three, and your knees against the crossbar or touching each other beneath it. Use your inside leg as a wind-break on the bends, bringing the inside pedal up and pushing your knee outwards. This will slow you down and help you around the bend with less braking. Once again, if you have to brake on a downhill bend, do the braking before the corner if possible, so you go through the trickiest part without having the brakes on.

On bends, follow a similar procedure to the one for taking bends on the flat, but allow for the

Descending Mont Ventoux, this string of riders shows the technique of lifting the inside knee and leaning through the bend.

fact that you are tackling them at a much higher speed, and with the benefit of gradient. Once you let off the brakes, you will immediately gain speed again.

Braking

The best way to brake well is to know your brakes. Have them adjusted so that they feel the same on your training and racing bikes, which means that the instinctive application of the brakes won't have a greater or lesser effect than you expect.

Remember that you have spent much energy in getting up speed, and you don't want to waste that energy by braking unnecessarily. During a race, brake as little as possible. Instead, just ease up on the pedals if you see a hazard looming up, and see if that's enough; then start to brake very gently, and only really brake hard if you have to.

You have two brakes, so use them both; but beware of braking too hard on the rear wheel, which will induce a skid on wet roads or fast bends. Better to spread the braking load over both wheels, and then you are less likely to lose control.

Make sure your brake levers are shaped and positioned so that you can apply them efficiently when riding on the brake hoods. If you can't do this adequately, then either re-position them or change the levers until you can.

If your front brake judders, then check whether your headset has worn loose. If not, then check the rim for a buckle. Fix it or change it. If your rear brake judders, then it must be a buckled wheel.

Gear-changing

The principles of using gears are much the same for a bike as for a car. Just as the car's engine likes to perform within a given range of revs, so your body is happier when your legs are spinning at a certain rhythm – the optimum RPM. Just as a car's engine starts to labour if it is in too high a gear, so you start to use your energy inefficiently when your bike is overgeared. It's just as bad when you are undergeared, too. So it is important to watch the terrain – and if possible to know it in advance – so you can get the best out of your gears.

Gear mechanisms work more positively when they are moving with their spring mechanisms – that is, changing up on the rear gear and down on the front changer. Changing your derailleur up should be a matter of 'clunk-clunk-clunk' or even 'click-click-click'. Changing down the rear mechanism produces a gentle clatter which only eases as you find the desired sprocket. But then you'll find that out for yourself as you do more gear-changing.

Because of the way your gears operate, you should avoid getting caught in a big gear when a rival attacks or a sprint is launched. It is a simple matter to flick into a bigger gear on the rear mechanism, but much more tricky to change down. In finishing sprints you should have selected your gear well in advance, but change up if you have to. Change down, and you've probably lost.

If a steep climb suddenly presents itself, reach for the left-hand lever and change to the small chainring, which should be quick and positive: drop the gear a considerable amount in just one movement. Far better to move on to the small ring early rather than later.

'Overchanging' – that is, changing too far up or down and easing back into the desired sprocket – shouldn't be necessary with a quality gear mechanism, whose action should be smooth and positive. Changing the rear mechanism needs a gentle touch, and improves with familiarity. Once you are used to a gear, it's better to stay with the same model when you replace it, or you'll have to find your touch all over again.

Occasionally you will unship your chain when changing chainwheels. It needn't be a disaster unless the chain has jammed firmly between the crank and large chainwheel. If you have derailed it towards the outside, then try moving your gear lever as if to change on to the small ring, but not all the way. Keep pedalling gently, and hope your front changer will pick up the chain and engage it on the outer ring again. Do the same in reverse if the chain is unshipped inwards. If this method works, it will work quickly. If it doesn't, dismount and do the job properly. If the rear gear changes too far to the outside and the chain jams between the smallest sprocket and the frame, you will have to stop to unjam it, and be careful with your changing until you can readjust the gear following the race.

Race craft

The reason why older and experienced roadmen who are past their best years can still survive with younger and fitter riders is their ability to save strength by clever riding. You can ride defensively to avoid making undue efforts, and you can ride aggressively to compel your rivals to make just such undue efforts, simply by placing yourself correctly in relation to other riders and with regard to the wind direction. Professional riders automatically take the best available shelter, accelerate and decelerate as gradually as the race situation will allow, relax whenever possible, and only make efforts when they have to. Learning how to do this instinctively is a matter of experience. But you can learn the principles here.

Following a wheel

If two riders are racing side by side with a headwind or a tailwind, they are putting out equal efforts. If one rider is behind the other, he will have the advantage of the leader's slipstream, and will use less energy to travel at the same speed. Making good use of this slipstream effect is the key to riding economically, and 'following a wheel' – or 'sitting in' – is an essential part of race craft.

The lead rider in a group is ploughing through the air, in just the same way as a boat ploughs through the water and leaves behind a 'wake' in a rapidly-widening V-shape. Anybody riding in this 'wake' receives some shelter

from the wind. The harder the headwind, or the faster the speed, the greater is the effect of the shelter, and the harder the lead rider must work in comparison with the riders following.

Assuming that the wind is coming from the front and not the side, then the most sheltered position is immediately behind the rider in front. However, since some riders will not be riding in a straight line, it is safer to ride, not directly behind, but slightly to one side or the other. Better, in fact, to ride slightly to the outside of the one in front, just in case he moves in and traps your front wheel against the kerb, even by accident. In any case, be wary of

Wheel-following in a fast-moving bunch. There are only a few inches between the back wheel of each rider and the front wheel of the rider behind. Note that the riders' eyes are not on the wheel in front, since they instinctively keep a constant distance behind. Instead, they watch the action of the racing.

overlapping with the rider in front, in case he moves out and touches your wheel. Be very aware of the problems that can be caused by wheels touching. If your front wheel touches the back wheel of the rider ahead, he will hardly notice, but you will have your work cut out to stay upright. So always keep an eye on the wheels in front of you, and give yourself a safety margin.

Echelon riding

The technique of wheel-following changes when the wind is coming from the side. When this happens, you seek shelter, not almost directly behind the lead rider, but at an angle corresponding to the direction of the wind, combined with the effect of forward motion. For example, if the wind were blowing directly from the side, then you would be riding, not alongside the other rider, but perhaps half a length back and to the leeward side. Your position will vary according to the angle of the wind, and with experience you will be able to feel the right place to ride in.

It follows from this that in a headwind a group of riders will be riding basically in line astern. In a sidewind of any kind, this formation takes more of an angle across the road, using whatever width is available. This formation is called an *echelon*. If the wind is coming from the right, then the rider on the right-hand side of the road is fully in the wind; all riders to the left of him are sheltered to some degree.

Let's consider this in relation to a big bunch. In a headwind, the bunch would normally become elongated, and would simply occupy more space from front to

Facing: The frenetic scene at the annual world pro road championship, which must be the ultimate goal of every road rider.

Above: The clean lines of the top-class road racing bike, here ridden by Holland's Joop Zoetemelk. This model is Italian, but in a style followed by makers all over the world.

Right: Promising young amateur Keith Reynolds is relaxed when cornering. Note that the inside knee is raised and the leg nearest the camera is slightly bent, even though the crank is vertical.

Previous page: The traditional cycling nations are now having to cede the honours to the New World. This is the American Greg Lemond, who won the world pro road championship in 1983.

A small group in echelon formation. The wind is blowing from the riders' right. The rider with the striped hat has just finished his turn at the front and is dropping back into a more sheltered position.

Sidewinds split up a big bunch into several echelons, each one using the full width of the road. The wind is blowing from the right-hand side. Note how the front echelon appears more disorganised, since more riders want to find a place in it. If all the strong men gather in the front echelon, it will gradually pull away from the others.

'Working'

Clearly, because of the slipstreaming effect in road racing, no one rider is going to be content to sit at the front of a bunch and take all the buffeting of the wind while the rest shelter behind him. So it is

A fast-moving bunch, with Dutchman Gerrie Knetemann doing a hard turn at the front. The riders behind him are ready to take their turn when he moves over.

Even two riders in a breakaway can work successfully. Here, in the 1983 Het Volk classic in Belgium, home rider Fons De Wolf leads Dutchman Jan Raas. De Wolf is just finishing his turn in front and has moved over for Raas to take the lead. The smaller the group, the longer the turns in front, to allow enough time for the sheltering rider or riders to recover.

back. But in a strong sidewind, the leading riders would form an echelon across the available width of the road. Let's assume that eight riders use up the whole width of the road – so where do the others go?

Rider number eight is in the left-hand gutter, but still sheltered by rider number seven. But rider number nine cannot move to the left of rider eight: there's no room. So he is left to ride in the left-hand gutter with minimal shelter. Number ten has the same problem, and so on. With an inexperienced field, you see an echelon forming a tail of riders grovelling in the gutter, hardly sheltered. Inevitably they fall back, having used up their strength at a far faster rate than those in the

Immaculate Italian Roberto Visentini, demonstrating modern race clothing.

echelon proper.

Not so with a field of experienced riders. In this situation, rider number nine would move to the right-hand side of the road and start a new echelon of his own, followed by numbers 10, 11 through to 16, and so on. The Dutch are past masters at this, coming from a country which is flat and often windswept. They call the echelon a *waaier*; the French call it a *bordure*.

Strong riders love it when the echelons form, because it allows them to use their strength against weaker riders. Often using shoulders and elbows, the tough men fight their way into the front echelon, and use strength and tactics to stay there. There is daylight between the echelons, and that daylight tends to grow, the stronger men at the front pulling away from the echelons behind.

the principle of riding in a bunch or group that everyone takes his turn at the front. This is called 'working', 'pulling', or doing 'bit and bit'.

Well, that's the principle, but it doesn't work out equally in practice. In fact, many riders in a bunch won't be doing their turn at the front, or perhaps will be doing a shorter turn than others. It might be that they are simply too tired to maintain the pace and prefer to shelter in the biggest part of the bunch, surrounded by many other riders. Or maybe they are simply saving themselves for later efforts. However, if they are in such a position, they are badly placed to react to any attacking moves.

The racing bunch

Seen from the air, a racing bunch has three distinct component parts:

1. About the first quarter of the field will be working, taking turns at the front and then swinging off to the side and easing back into a

During the 1983 world amateur championships, this bunch is working hard. The right-hand file is of riders moving forward, while the left-hand file, led by rider 244, is of riders who have recently done their bit at front and are easing back to a sheltered position.

sheltered position. Generally speaking, turns at the front last for around 20 pedal revs, which means that at any one time the working riders form a kind of continuous rotating chain, half of them moving forwards towards taking their turn at the front, the others easing backwards until they reach the end of the chain and move forwards again. These are the riders in contention, who really affect the racing. They are expending more energy than those behind them, but at least they can make or join a break when they choose.

A bird's-eye view of a bunch. Clearly the active part is at the front, where only a few riders seem very interested in making the pace. Most riders seem content to sit in the wider part of the bunch and enjoy a sheltered ride.

2. Behind these riders are those who have chosen not to work at all or to work only occasionally. They are the prisoners of their own decision.

3. At the back of the bunch there are generally a few who are finding it hard even to maintain the speed of the field, despite being sheltered. They will gradually have fallen back from the belly of the bunch to the rear, and are at the mercy of any sudden acceleration. When the speed goes up, gaps open, and the weaker riders cannot close them. The back of the bunch is not a happy place to be.

The 'workers' will behave differently depending on their motives. Some may have reasons to work harder or longer at the front: perhaps they are wholeheartedly chasing a breakaway, or they have no finishing sprint and are trying to draw the sting of other riders who have.

Others may go 'through and off', which means they take their place at the head of the field only for a rev or two, and then swing across to let the next man through. Such riders may wish to remain in an alert position near the head of the bunch, but want to save their strength for later efforts. Perhaps they are unsure of their ability to stay the pace if they work wholeheartedly. So they 'soft-tap', but don't actually hinder progress.

Still others in the working section will be hindering progress – 'blocking'. This happens when they have a team-mate in a breakaway in front, and want to give him the best chance to stay away. Or perhaps it's the reverse situation: they have a team-mate who is delayed by a puncture, and want to dislocate the progress of the bunch so that he can catch up more easily.

Whatever the reason, blocking tactics aren't welcomed. Riders who block will be shouted at, leaned on, and generally given a difficult time. Such riders have ended up, quite mysteriously, in a ditch, on frequent occasions. Blocking is, however, a legitimate team tactic, and is practised quite unmercifully by the Eastern European nations, for whom team racing is quite a science. In the Milk Race, when the Russians were dominating, it was quite normal to see four or five red jerseys massed at the front of the field when they had a man or two in the breakaway. Four or five big strong men at the front can take quite some dislodging!

In echelons, riders also 'work', and this happens in one of two ways. If the echelon is well clear of the rest, and has no 'tail' of riders hoping to find themselves a place in it, then the rider in the wind simply finishes his turn at the front, eases, and slips across behind the other riders to join the echelon at the other end (see right). No problems here.

If there is a 'tail', however, it happens differently. Clearly those in the echelon will want to keep the riders in the 'tail' from taking their place as they move across the rest. So instead of slipping across behind, the rider first moves forwards, and then passes gradually across the front wheels of the others until he reaches the opposite gutter; then he eases, and drops into the sheltered slot. The riders in the 'tail' can't get in, because their front wheels are more vulnerable than the echelon-rider's rear wheel, so they have to give way as he slips backwards towards them (see far right).

A normal echelon, showing the path taken by a rider after doing his turn at the front

A defensive echelon, where the relieved rider must kick forward and across the front of the other riders – with great care and plenty of clearance

The bunch versus the lone rider

Given the slipstreaming effect, and the effect of many riders working together, it would seem theoretically impossible that a lone rider, or a small group, could ever break away from the bunch and stay clear to the finish. Indeed, many events on flat courses finish with mass sprints, particularly when there is a good following wind. But

there are other factors to take into account.

Occasionally there are riders of such ability – super-champions like Fausto Coppi or Eddy Merckx, or riders of talent working their way up through the categories fast – that they only need to open daylight between themselves and the rest, perhaps on a hill or on a sharp bend, to have enough advantage on which to build a lone victory. Alone,

climbing inevitably reduces the speed, making the slipstream effect less critical.

This would appear to indicate that races can only be won by the extremely talented, or by good finishing sprinters. But happily this is not so. The rider of average physical ability can still win if he has tactical sense coupled with luck. Lone breaks by less significant riders can succeed if made at the right moment. Similarly, breakaway groups containing no race favourites can produce winning moves if they are made at the right time. It all depends on apathy and fatigue.

When a bunch is chasing hard, all the riders at the front are participating in the effort, as in this Milk Race shot. It means a tough time for any breakaway.

they can ride faster than a chasing bunch of riders working flat out.

There are other riders too who are not necessarily super-champions, but who are able to generate a supreme effort over perhaps ten kilometres – enough to keep them away from the rest of the field if they make this effort within that distance of the finish.

Still others are brilliant climbers, and can open big gaps on long ascents, hoping to hold their advantage to the finish. This, of course, depends on whether the climb in question is near enough to the finish for them to do this. It is precisely to encourage such top

climbers that mountain-top finishes are included in the Tour de France and the Giro d'Italia.

Riders with such talents are usually well known, and are 'marked' by their rivals accordingly. Because of the slipstreaming effect, such riders must first open reasonable daylight between themselves and the next man to stand a chance of succeeding. Otherwise, they will only succeed in leading a conga of nicely-sheltered riders, and expending their strength uselessly. Every such rider should find himself 'marked' by his main rivals or their team-mates. The better the rider, the more immediate must be the reaction to his breakaway attempt, because he must not be allowed to get properly clear.

Only the born climber really has a chance of 'riding the rest off his wheel' by sheer uphill speed, since

Contrast the Milk Race shot with this one of the bunch in a rainy Liège-Bastogne-Liège. The bunch stretches right across the road, and no one seems keen on making the pace. In such circumstances a breakaway could gain much ground very quickly.

Making a break

If you watch the progress of a road race, it separates into periods of varying activity at the front of the bunch. Early in the race, such activity is frisky but hardly serious: few believe in the ability of themselves or any other rider to stay away this early.

Then the race is really on and attacking begins in earnest. The seriousness of the pursuit matches the seriousness of the attack, because those who are able to affect the race will judge that now is the time to attack, join or counter the efforts of other attackers. Such serious periods of attacking are often provoked by hills or stretches of rough roads, because the very terrain will rule some riders out of serious chasing efforts.

Once an attack has succeeded in opening a margin of a minute, activity at the head of the bunch often settles down, either to a steady chasing effort, or to a resigned plod if it appears that the breakaway is uncatchable.

Towards the finish, activity increases again, whether or not there is an existing break, as riders unsure of their finishing sprint ability try to steal away from the established sprinters. Then there is often a slight lull before the wind-up to a grandstand bunch finish.

All this is predictable – but only the good tactician can pick the moment to attack which will not attract a big chasing effort. The best time to attack is when the majority of riders are less inclined to take up the chase, for whatever reason. Here are some occasions when such conditions exist:

1. When a dangerous breakaway is just about to be reeled in after a hard chase. The breakaway rider or group has realised that the chance is over, and is easing to be caught. When the gap is reduced to only a few yards, sprint across it and keep your effort going. You may pick up some of the stronger breakaway riders, while the slower ones dropping back towards the bunch will hinder any immediate reaction from behind.

A breakaway from a breakaway. Seeing a chasing group obviously about to overhaul his breakaway group, Aussie Phil Anderson attacks hard, and only one other man goes with him. The chasers caught the rest of the group, but Anderson went on to win alone.

2. Just before, or just over, the top of a long climb. Again, the bunch will have made a big effort to climb it and to contain the climbing specialists – and will naturally want to ease at the summit. If you take a flyer when they are thinking of taking a breather, the gap will be much more easily opened. But don't try this tactic if the descent follows immediately after the summit and you are a lousy descender.

The pace is fast up this hill, so it is hard for anyone to break clear. But at the top of the climb, as everyone naturally eases, there will be a good chance.

3. When the bunch appear to be more interested in eating and drinking. This often happens after a break has been caught. As if by some telepathic agreement, hands reach for drinking bottles or into back pockets for food. Now is the moment to attack, since all those eaters and drinkers will have to clear the tables before they can react.

The bunch in a playful mood. At such times there is likely to be very little reaction to a breakaway attempt. Such periods are usually found soon after the start of any race, when there is still plenty of time left to bring back any breaks.

4. When there is a crash. This may seem unsporting, but the fact that you haven't been caught up in the crash is a legitimate benefit of good placement in the bunch or of good riding. Some riders will be down, others baulked; still others will be team-mates of the crashed riders and more occupied with *their* fate than with chasing you. Give it everything.

A crash – a signal to break away. It will eliminate or delay many of your rivals.

5. When good riders are off the back because of punctures or mechanical trouble. Their team-mates will be falling back to help them, and thus unable to chase you.

6. When the roads are twisting and narrow. This means that the bunch must string out, and only the riders at or near the front of the field will be able to react to an attack. Many of those behind won't even be able to see it, let alone react.

7. On a bend, attacking either into the bend or out of it. Once again, only the leading riders will be able to react, and those behind will, because of the whiplash effect explained earlier, have even more difficulty reacting.

42

The road is narrow and winding. For those at the back of the bunch, any breakaways are difficult to see and impossible to chase.

The actual mechanics of making a break are relatively simple: the aim is to create as big a gap as possible in the shortest possible time.

On open roads, don't attack from the front, because everyone is

Breaking away from the front is rarely successful. The second rider has no difficulty countering this move.

following the leader and will find it easy to just match your acceleration. All you will achieve is to string out the bunch and wear yourself out prematurely. The best position for launching an attack is from a few places back in the bunch. In a small group this can even be last place in that group.

Go from a position where you will have a clear run. Believe in yourself: use a gear somewhat larger than normal for the speed of the bunch; get out of the saddle and launch yourself into action in the shortest time possible.

To overtake the handful of riders in front, you should either pass on the other side of the road (if road conditions and safety permit), or else come whistling past their ears. In the first case they will have to switch sideways to gain your slipstream. In the second case they will involuntarily shy away and their reaction time will be delayed. As you pass them, you should be moving at a much higher speed than they are, so that the gap will be open before they react.

Resist the temptation to look round for at least 30 seconds. Looking back will cause you to lose momentum, and may be just enough to allow the chasing riders to tack on to your back wheel and cancel out your attack.

After that initial period of do-or-die effort, you may just be able to judge the reaction without looking round. The familiar breathing and gear-rattle of the bunch may be around your ears again, in which case ease back and watch for counter-attacks.

If your ears tell you that you have shed all or most of your pursuers, sneak a look back under your armpit (yes – it does work, try it!).

A breakaway at the moment of consolidation. The bunch is about 30 seconds behind, and there are at least two further groups trailing them. This three-man breakaway includes two riders from the Peugeot team. This gives them a natural advantage over the third member, who may decide that third place is better than none, or may elect not to work because he is outnumbered. The rider behind is Scotland's Robert Millar.

Incidentally, if there is a rider on your wheel who feels particularly aggressive, he might wait for you to look under your armpit and then immediately attack you on the blind side (if he doesn't fancy your company in a break, that is).

Having looked back, take stock of the situation. If the gap isn't big enough, give it one more go if you have the breath: it might be enough to break the resistance of the chase just when they think they've got you.

If the gap *is* big enough, settle down to time trialling: relax, and concentrate on getting a good rhythm; pick a good line on the road and watch for the best surfaces, particularly on rutted and cobbled roads. The next goal is to get out of sight, which, on an average road with the occasional bend, requires a gain of over a minute. Once you are out of sight of your pursuers, the gap will often grow faster, because they lose heart, and do not know how fast you are going.

You may get time checks on the pursuit from motorcycle marshals, from commissaires' cars, or from your team vehicle. Make your tactical decisions on the basis of whether your lead is growing, and if so how fast. If you are away alone, you must be riding at a speed you

expect to be able to maintain to the finish. Knowing the terrain, and the direction of the route in relation to the wind, will help you decide if you can hang on or not.

If time checks show a pursuing group coming up very fast, then ease if you aren't confident of staying away to the finish. This also means you will be better able to go with them when they catch you up.

You look behind and find that you've opened a gap on the bunch but there are a few other riders with you? Well, that's fine, unless one of them is an 'undesirable' whom for team reasons you wouldn't want as part of your breakaway.

Assessing the worth of such a breakaway group is part of good road racing, and presupposes a knowledge of your rivals and their relative strengths. You are looking for a group big enough to consolidate a break against a chasing bunch, but not so big that a good working rhythm can't be found. The group needs to be big enough so that each man can put in a solid turn at the front and then have time to recover in the slipstream of the others until his turn comes round again. In effect this is possible with as few as four riders if the bunch isn't too keen on chasing – but six or eight is better. Any more than this tends to be non-productive, as some riders will start to think they can take an easy ride.

Anyway, let's suppose that you look under your armpit to see six pairs of eyes staring at you from under six crash-hats, and that an unspoken alliance is instantly formed.

You've done your initial share of the work by launching the break. Ease to the right if the wind is from

This breakaway (above) seems to be losing steam. With nine riders comprising it, the move does not have any great urgency about it – which is the problem with numerically strong breaks.

Contrast with this five-man break-away in a British professional event (below). They are all contributing to the effort and committed to its success. Such a group would hold off an apathetic bunch.

the right and vice versa, and let the other riders come past – but only gradually. Watch for the last man to come past and ease into his slipstream. Try to relax, change down a gear, get your breath back and start to assess the others.

See the guy in the lead? He's freewheeling, so obviously has no interest in keeping the break going – probably the opposite. Maybe he has a team leader stuck back in the bunch and he's blocking. The rider behind has to sprint around him to pick up the pace again, and the blocking rider won't be allowed to take the lead again without a struggle.

There's another rider at the front now, and no sooner is he at the head of the string then he has eased sideways and is coming back towards you. He's not blocking, but he's not really contributing much either. Too many soft-tappers like this and the break is doomed to failure. He isn't 'working', and as such is breaking the rule that riders should contribute to the pace-making in a breakaway. Such riders get shouted at, jostled, ridden into the gutter. Life isn't easy.

But give him a chance. Perhaps he made such an effort to join the break that he needs to recuperate before he can begin to work properly. If that's the case he'll soon say so, and then begin to contribute.

If a break lasts a long time, its members tend to develop a kind of comradeship. If one rider has minor trouble – perhaps pulls his foot out of the toe-clip on a climb or loses ground – the others are likely to wait for him. Only towards the finish are such incidents capitalised upon. For the time being, having an extra rider to share the work is more important

than eliminating a rival.

You won't always feel strong in a break. Your reserves might dip and you might be the one soft-tapping while you seek to recuperate, all the while taking small amounts of food and drink to try to lift your blood-sugar level. Your companions will allow such rests for a while, and then will start to make life uncomfortable for you. Are you perhaps stronger than you say? Are you saving your strength for the finishing sprint, or for a lone attempt to split the break and leave the others who have done their share of work? Sometimes road racing has elements of poker.

There are ways of eliminating riders who don't work. Once they are at the back of the string they see the rider in front allow a gap to open. To close it they must sprint around the rider in front, who simply picks up the speed again to keep himself in the break. If this happens every time the offender is at the back, the message starts to get through. They must work or else they will be compelled to make effort after effort to conserve any chance of winning.

Nearing the finish

As the final kilometres roll by, the bunch behind either will have given up the chase or will be redoubling its efforts to pull back the break. In the latter case, the breakaway riders are virtually forced to work together until the finishing sprint starts, for fear that any finessing (cat-and-mouse tactics) will result in their being caught. If, however, it is clear that the break will be able to stay clear until the finish, riders will often seek to turn the odds in their favour by cutting down the opposition.

A good sprinter will be happy for the break to stay together, because he will be confident of his ability to win. Therefore he will make no efforts to split the group up before the finish.

On the other hand, any rider without a finishing sprint will have to resign himself to finishing last of the group unless he can split it or leave

On the final hill of the Liège-Bastogne-Liège, a strong climber sees his chance. In the first picture, Dutchman Stefan Rooks looks behind to see his breakaway companions in difficulty. He switches across the road to open a big gap very quickly, and carries on to win alone.

the others behind. So he will be attacking from a group in much the same way as he might have launched the attack from the original bunch. With a smaller group, the element of surprise is harder to achieve, but the element of fatigue is more pronounced. Near the finish, riders will be near the end of their strength and any difference in fitness levels will be more evident. Given the right terrain and the right timing of an effort, a strong rider can ride right away from his tiring rivals.

Even tired sprinters can usually outsprint strong non-sprinters because of their talent in raising a short effort. So the strong non-sprinter must try his utmost to leave them behind before the final kilometre.

If you feel strong, then it won't hurt to test out your companions with a half-power effort on a rise or other difficult terrain. Let them believe this was your best effort, and sag back into their company again – but only after having noted which riders reacted fastest and strongest, for these are your real rivals. Bear in mind that they too might be play-acting to conceal how, strong they are. Watch for their breathing; see how strong are their turns at the front after your effort, and decide if or when it is worth attacking again.

The sprint

Finishing sprints can be long or short. With a big bunch the sprint tends to wind up to a high speed from perhaps ten kilometres out, the non-sprinters in a team keeping the pace high so that no one can jump away. Meanwhile the sprint specialists will be working their way gradually towards the front, usually on the back wheel of a team-mate assigned for that purpose.

Such a team-mate gives what is called a 'lead-out'. He is leading the sprinter up through the bunch, gradually picking up the speed until he hits the last kilometre virtually flat out and very near the head of the bunch. As the lead-out man's strength ebbs, he eases across (towards the source of any sidewind) and leaves the sprinter to launch his own final effort.

The essential is for the sprint-finish specialist to stay in shelter for as long as possible. If his lead-out man fades too early, he might instead switch across into the shelter of a rival sprinter and use *his* slipstream until the last moment. As you will quickly discover, this isn't an easy manoeuvre, especially if the chosen sheltering sprinter has other team-mates protecting his back wheel!

In big-bunch sprints of international races like the Tour de France, teams have developed to a fine art the process of getting their man up to the front – so much so that the same riders tend to occupy the leading positions in one bunch sprint after another. Only the order might change slightly. So learn from them – and if you have a team to back you or a sprinter in your team worth working for, make sure you have a sprint drill rehearsed beforehand.

In small-group sprints, with little or no supporting team involvement, the actual sprint can be very short indeed: no single rider wants to act as lead-out man for the rest, and consequently ruin his own chances. So the break goes slower and slower until someone's nerve

cracks. It isn't unusual to see riders attempt a standstill like track sprinters, and then explode into action over the last 200 metres or so.

Whether the sprint is from a big bunch or from a small group, there are certain basic principles which apply.

Firstly, stay in the most sheltered position for as long as possible. This means finding a good back wheel – preferably that of your danger-man – and only moving out into the wind to make your final effort. Try this in training, sprinting from the front and then the back position, and you'll see what a difference such shelter makes.

The finishing sprint is often at the highest speed reached during the race, and therefore the effect of wind resistance is also at its greatest. Be conscious not only of the best wheel to follow when the sprint starts, but also whether the wind is coming from one side or the other. Always try to come off a wheel on the sheltered side.

The second principle is to choose the right gear for the sprint – and here it is important to have reconnoitred the finish area in advance if possible, or at the very least to have studied the plan of the finish area if one is provided. If the wind is against you, if the finish is uphill, or if the distance from the last corner to the line is very short: then you should consider reducing your gear from the norm. If, however, there's a following or a neutral wind, or if there's a big bunch and the finish is at the end of a kilometre-long straight on flat or descending roads, then you should gear up.

There is nothing worse than having to change gear once the final

effort is launched; but if you have to guess on a gear, err on the small side rather than the large. It is much easier on the gear mechanism to snick into a higher gear than into a lower one when the chain is under full tension.

Thirdly, make sure you have somewhere to go. Don't allow too many riders in front of you during the wind-up for the finish. Don't imagine that, just because you are finishing faster, those in front will graciously move over to let you through. It won't happen.

On the run-in, be aware of your opposition: roughly where in the bunch are the other good sprinters, and what are their colours? If one of them decides to make an early move – too early in your opinion – try to get over on to his wheel.

Try to place yourself where you won't be forced into the wind prematurely to pass another rider. Conversely, try to put your rivals in the worst position. If the wind is coming from the right-hand side of the road (and assuming that the finish is traffic-free), then a rider in the left-hand gutter knows that he can only be passed on the right, so that anyone passing him will be 'in the wind'. However, be aware also that crowds lining the finish can cut off the effect of a crosswind.

For similar reasons, watch for road surfaces. If you can sprint on a smooth patch and leave your rivals the cobbles, then you have the advantage.

Assess each finishing sprint in relation to your rivals. If you feel you are the strongest and the finish is uphill into the wind, then launch a long sprint. This should hopefully tire out those sprinter rivals who in a short sprint might just be able to muster the leg-speed to get past you

Conversely, if you are tired but are otherwise a talented sprinter, then do your best to engineer a short sprint. It's not unusual to see a sprint finisher in terrible trouble over the closing kilometres, yo-yoing on and off the back on each hill, but then coming through to win, thanks to his outstanding sprinting talent – a burst of speed which he can always sustain over a short period. This is why the strongest rider is not always the winner.

If you are a no-hoper in the sprint, try for surprise. Jump away before anyone expects it, and certainly before 200 metres to go. It's just possible that the established sprinters will expect you to fade and be caught before the line. They might be more interested in watching each other, thus enabling you to win before they can react.

You can learn a lot about sprinting on the road by visiting your local track and watching the tactics used there. Note that the top track sprinters never use a fantastically high gear, 90 inches (say 50 x 15) being typical. Although you will have to get out of the saddle to get your gear moving in a short sprint, your final acceleration will depend on a fast pedalling rate, and this can only reach its maximum while you are in the saddle again. You rarely see top road sprinters finishing out of the saddle, unless they have overgeared and the finish is harder than expected. Instead, they imitate their track 'brothers', thrusting the handlebars forward with outstretched arms and head down, 'throwing' the bike forward at the last moment to gain those few extra inches. This technique needs to be practised, since mistiming it can cause you to lose ground.

Puncture drill

Many races now have service cars and team cars following, so a puncture need not be the disaster it used to be.

If you realise you have punctured, don't announce the fact to anyone but your team-mates. If you are a danger-man to others, they will accelerate as soon as they know you are in trouble; so don't tell them. Let a team-mate know, and gently ease your way to the back of the bunch. As you near the back, lift your arm high to let the people in the service car know. Look behind to make sure they have seen and are moving up to

The sprint finish to the 1982 Amstel Gold Race. Phil Anderson (background) has already settled for third place in this sprint, leaving the battle between Irishman Sean Kelly (left) and Germany's Gregor Braun. Kelly lunges at the line with his arms straight out, but has mistimed his effort. Braun's arms are still in the act of pushing the bike forward, and are gaining those vital centimetres.

help. Change into top gear; pull to the side of the road, both for safety and for the convenience of the service car. This should be on the left-hand side in the UK and on the right-hand side in countries where they drive on the right; on closed roads follow race regulations.

If the service mechanic is within sight or earshot, let him know by gesture or voice which wheel is affected. Point, shout or do both. If the mechanic is close by, remain astride the bike, with both feet on the ground, and allow him to lift the affected wheel and change it. If he's not close enough to give immediate help, then take the offending wheel out yourself and put it on the verge.

Once the new wheel is in, the mechanic should give you a good push-off. Now the vital task is to get back to the bunch or group as quickly as possible. Every moment you are out on your own will sap your strength. Better an all-out effort than an attempt to work your way back gradually. Hopefully your team-mates will help, unless their team priorities are with another rider

No point in dismounting for this puncture. Phil Anderson stands patiently astride his machine while the mechanic changes the wheel.

and it's near the finish.

When a rider punctures, one team-mate stays near the back of the bunch and keeps an eye out for the puncture victim to appear in full chase. Depending on the situation, he might start to drop back even before he sees the chasing rider.

He should ease gradually, keeping pedalling at a good rate. The chaser should not tack gratefully on to his back wheel, but instead should go straight by without slackening speed. Only when the team-mate has accelerated into his slipstream should the chaser ease to the back and take a well-earned rest. If necessary, other team-mates will drop back at intervals, so that the two-man chasing group becomes three, four and so on, with every extra rider increasing the chances of getting back safely.

The aim is to get back to the bunch; but once the chasers have reached the column of following cars, they can at least take a breather in the shelter offered. Be aware of race regulations, and only ride immediately behind the car if this is generally practised. Otherwise, riding alongside also gives a considerable amount of shelter.

Once you reach the tail of the bunch, don't assume the task is finished. The tail-enders get a very rough ride, and there are often splits which can send you quickly off the back again. Better to move right up into the front third of the field, where the bunch is broadest and the shelter is good. Then re-assess the situation and concentrate on recuperating before making your next move.

Stage racing

Stage racing is so called because the event is split into stages and usually lasts more than one day. It can mean a two-stage one-day race, or an event like the Tour de France, which lasts almost a month, has more than 20 stages, and includes a couple of rest days. Each stage is a separate race with its own prizes, but the main prize list is for the 'general classification' – the result when each rider's times for all the stages are totalled. The shortest overall time wins, of course.

This means that, as the race progresses, the riders taking part have two priorities: one is to try to win or perform well on each particular stage; the other – more important as the race nears its conclusion – is to ride in support of the team's best-placed rider or riders overall.

Team tactics are applied much more in stage racing than in one-day races. After all, in a one-day race every man starts with a theoretically equal chance of winning. In a stage race, the pattern taken by the general classification means that at the start of every stage certain riders have a better chance of overall victory, simply by virtue of what they have done in the stages so far. Added to this, certain riders are reckoned to have little chance overall because they are not strong in, for instance, climbing. In the Tour de France, which traditionally starts with flat stages dominated by the sprint-finish specialists, the general classification only really starts to take on a definitive look once the

first mountain stages have been ridden. By this time the flat-road specialists have lost so much time that only those who have performed well in the mountains can be in with an overall chance.

The good climbers and those with all-round talent are therefore worthy of the fullest possible team support, which comes in many forms. If they puncture, for instance, they are likely to be handed a team-mate's bike while he waits for a spare wheel. When a rival breaks away, it is the team-mates who chase and drag the bunch up to cancel out the breakaway, while the protected rider sits safely in the shelter of the bunch, waiting for the moment to launch or go with an attack. When that happens, the team-mates – often called 'domestiques', even in English cycling jargon – go to the front of the bunch and try to block the pursuit. If the protected rider needs a drink, a team-mate gives up his bottle. Over climbs, the protected rider may feel a surreptitious helping push to ease his progress over the tough parts. This is because, when the racing really gets tough, he is expected to produce the goods and win, for the honour – and equally-divided profit – of the team.

In big teams there may be two or three protected riders. Sometimes one of the domestiques might join a break, then do no work in it or try to block its progress in vain – and the break might gain so much time that he becomes highly placed overall. In such circumstances fate earns him a measure of protection.

To a well-informed team rider, the task becomes easier as a stage race progresses and some of the expected rivals drop out of the overall reckoning. In the end, there

Rider 123 is Bernard Hinault, the leader of La Vie Claire's team. He has eased off the back of the bunch to take off some unwanted clothing, but will soon find team-mates waiting to pace him back up to the leaders again.

are perhaps only half a dozen riders who represent a threat, and only they are relentlessly chased down when they attack. Towards the end of a stage race, the overall victory and supporting places are often so sharply defined that there is an unofficial truce between the top riders, and the domestiques are given a chance to show what they can do to win a stage on their own.

In stage racing, it is said, the winner is the man who never has a bad day. Sometimes an overall winner doesn't even win a stage, but is consistently placed every day, and is always to the fore in the mountain stages when there can be big gains and losses in time.

In the Tour de France, the Giro d'Italia, in the US Coors Classic, and in England's pro-am Milk Race, riders are stretched to the limit, not only physically, but mentally too. Sometimes they are stretched too much, and their bodies develop problems such as boils or rashes which eventually ruin their chances.

It is on a stage race that team officials really come into their own. It is their job to free the riders from all the worries of the race which have nothing to do with the actual riding itself. (When you go to a one-day race you naturally expect to have to prepare your own bike, clothes and race food, and you decide 'in the saddle' how you will ride the race.)

A typical stage-race team will have a team manager, who will organise race tactics, and take care of the administrative details of the events, such as making sure documentation is correct, passing race information on to riders, and arguing any protests.

The team soigneur will work on the riders' bodies and minds, to make sure that both are fit for the next day's stage. He will give a massage after each stage, attend to minor injuries, work with the race doctor on minor injuries or illnesses, and look after hotel accommodation and race feeding; one aspect of his role that is often overlooked is that of giving each rider a chance, usually while on the massage plinth, to unburden himself of any personal worries he might have.

The mechanic will overhaul and clean each bike after every stage, change the gear ratios to suit the following day's terrain, and often travel with the race to provide service in case of punctures or other mechanical problems. If you have any mechanical worries, or need gear modifications, warn the mechanic as early as possible.

A good team without good officials will perform at less than its potential. The officials help to smooth away the cares of racing, day after day, and the manager in

particular will help to guide riders' thoughts on tactics. In single-day races you always compete with a personal win in mind. In stage races the general interests of the team are paramount; a particular dedication and discipline of mind is required if you are told you must race purely to aid another rider, and not on your own account.

A good team mechanic can do wonders, even in the middle of a race!

Road racing is the most demanding of cycle-racing events and the most complex. It demands strength, speed, skill and stamina, and a weakness in any department will let the whole performance down. It demands the talents of track racing – but over a long period – and the ability to sprint and pursuit. The top roadman must be a top time triallist too, otherwise he can never hope to sustain a lone break. And it demands a constant mental output to adapt to the changing circumstances within any given event, for each move demands an instant decision whether to go with it or ride against it. Every race has a character all of its own, and therefore presents a fresh challenge.

3   *Time trialling*

Not for nothing has the time trial been called the 'race of truth' by cycling enthusiasts over the decades. Time trialling is the ultimate test of training, setting one man and his machine against his rivals over a given course on a given day, without the 'interference' of tactics. The winner of the time trial is the man who can go fastest or farthest over the prescribed course.

The 'set' distances in Britain – where time trialling has as many devotees as road racing and thus is more popular than elsewhere – are 10, 15, 25, 30, 50 and 100 miles, plus trials over 12 and 24 hours. In the last two events it is naturally the distance which counts.

Stage races also have time-trial prologues and time-trial stages, so time trialling is part of the road-racing scene too. They can vary from perhaps a kilometre to a couple of hours. Stage races may also include team time trials, in which members of a team ride together like a road-race breakaway, sharing the pace.

The glamorous face of time trialling, as part of a stage race. Here Malcolm Elliott hammers around the circuit at Sheffield during the 1984 Sealink International.

The time-trial bike

Because time-trial courses vary, so will time-trial bikes, for they tend to be more specialised than road-racing machines.

A road-racing bicycle will do quite nicely, of course; but since most courses are flat you will need close-ratio gears, and can therefore dispense with one of the chainwheels, leaving five, six or seven gears.

For time trials on flat courses with good road surfaces, the classic machine has a much shorter wheelbase and hence steeper angles. Wheels for such courses go

The classic short-distance time-trialling position, demonstrated by Eddie Adkins. On a short-wheelbase bike, and using a big gear with a single chainring, Adkins has moved forward until he is sitting on the point of the saddle.

51

down to 28 spokes, and large-flange hubs are much more common. Tyres also have smooth treads, since there is no great cornering element, and silk tubulars are also favoured if the weather is clement.

Gears tend to be larger, since time-trial stars have developed the ability to 'roll' the gear and hence turn it more slowly than the roadman, who needs high revs for greater flexibility. The time triallist can see up the road ahead and has no tactics or breakaway attempts to disturb his concentration. Therefore, as the gears go up, the revs come down, and longer cranks come into their own. Although many ordinary time triallists adopt a length of 170mm, the number of cranks of 175mm or even longer is growing fast. This can in some cases lead to knee problems in the first few events, because of the larger diameter of the pedalling circle.

Lightness is generally sought after, since the style of time trialling is not generally rough on bicycles, and corners are few, so that the tortional stresses are not so great as in a typical road race.

Of course, there are time trials on hilly courses and those which demand a great degree of bike-handling, and the machines used here will be very similar to the classic road-racing machine.

Position

This is very similar to the classic road position, except that the saddle can be a touch higher, to tip the rider forward. Usually racing is done on the dropped part of the handlebars, which also makes for a more aerodynamic position.

Big-gear users either sit further forward in relation to the bottom bracket, or 'self-adapt' their positions by sliding forward on to the tip of the saddle.

Clothing

Since speed is of the essence, streamlined clothing is important. In time trials where it is not necessary to carry food, top time triallists wear body-hugging skinsuits. The alternative is to wear skinshorts with a close-fitting silk 'track jersey', which amounts to the same thing. Beware, however, of early-morning and early-season events, where the weather may be so cold that wool shorts and a road-racing jersey might be preferable.

In longer time trials road-racing garb can be adopted, and the pockets can be used for food. Crash helmets are not necessary unless the particular event regulation requires their use.

Shoes should be close-fitting, and can be worn without socks for a better contact between shoe and foot, providing that the shoes fit well and do not chafe. Pay particular attention to foot care. Some laceless streamlined shoes are available.

Further aerodynamic aids which are becoming popular are Lycra-type hoods and arm coverings, designed so as to create a smoother outline.

Technique

The technique of time trialling revolves around concentration. Unlike in road racing, where the effects of a moment's inattention can be corrected later, in time trialling *any* time lost is lost for ever. For this reason you must develop a positive attitude towards every moment on the road.

Concentrate on keeping your gear turning smoothly at whatever you find to be your optimum revs. If you are a smooth pedaller, you will probably be doing over 100rpm; if you are a powerful rider and using bigger gears, then you may be down to 90 or even 80rpm. But as your revs drop, you need to make sure you are pulling up consciously on the pedals once the downstroke has been completed. This is a technique you can develop during training by riding for a while using the power from only one leg and just letting the other one be carried round by the revolution of the cranks. Make sure you give each leg a practice.

Concentrate on following a straight line relative to the road direction. If you find the bike is not following a straight track, you are probably using too big a gear, or possibly sitting too high.

Cut corners where possible to follow the shortest course, providing that the line you take isn't through any material which might cause punctures, or over any rough surface. Most time-trialling bikes don't like rough surfaces, and your progress is likely to be upset by any bump you hit.

Make sure that your riding position is aerodynamic. Keep your elbows tucked in, your back as near horizontal as possible, and your head still. Keep your head up sufficiently to see ahead.

Theoretically, the time triallist should be always at maximum speed for the road and weather conditions. In practice, since average speed tends to slow down as distance increases, maximum or near-maximum speed can only be held for a given time, until you start to work anaerobically (i.e. go into 'oyxgen debt'), and you have to ease. (This is explained in Chapter 7.) The ideal time triallist will work aerobically for most of his race, but on the edge of the anaerobic state. He will go into oxygen debt briefly to keep his speed going over the tops of hills, until the downward gradient starts to help him recover; and of course he will be working anaerobically during his finishing effort.

With properly balanced training you will gradually increase the speed at which you go into oxygen debt (the anaerobic threshold), so your times for a given distance will come down. For the average fit rider, there can be no question of 'pacing yourself' for distances below 50 miles. The body can normally go for almost two hours on its stores of glycogen, so all you need to do is find that anaerobic threshold and keep nudging at it throughout the race.

First you will need to warm up properly. Wrap up well, and warm up for half an hour or so. If you intend using a skinsuit, put on the bottom part and leave the top part hanging behind you; put on an extra jersey (or maybe two) over your undervest, and start your warm-up session. Arrange the end of the session to leave you enough time to take off your warm-up clothing, change your undervest, put your

The unruffled time-trial start of Bernard Hinault.

skinsuit on properly and put embrocation on your legs. Visit the toilet as near the starting time as possible.

The long warm-up, at gradually increasing speeds, will make it easy for your body to answer the demands of the explosive time trial start. Without the warm-up, your body will react adversely to this sudden intrusion on its normal rhythm: you will quickly find yourself gasping and have to ease to let your body catch up.

Once you have covered the first mile, you will be starting to settle down, and looking up the road for the rider who started in front of you. Never look behind to see who might be coming up behind: it only loses time and gains nothing.

After the start you will have moved up the gears to find the 'right' one for your speed potential. For the first few minutes, stay in a gear which brings you near to your maximum revs – which is kinder to your muscles. Then try to coax them into more effort and slightly fewer revs. Your body is amazingly good at beating its own private rhythm. 'Feel' the pedalling rhythm, and consciously try to increase it gradually until your legs and heart start to protest. If they don't protest, and the revs get much faster, change up a gear and repeat the process until you are turning the biggest gear possible for the conditions, and at your ideal personal rate of pedalling.

Don't let your attention be diverted, perhaps by wondering who is coming in the opposite direction or how far it is to the finish. If you don't know, don't waste time wondering!

If you are catching a rider, concentrate on him and once again try to lift the speed. If you have no rider in sight, then lift the speed as if sprinting for a distant point, then try to hold it. It will hurt, but probably not too much.

On hills, don't let your revs drop too much. If the hill is short and not too steep, get out of the saddle and try to sprint over the top. You can lose a lot of time by running out of steam just before the top of the climb and toiling over the top. Husband your energy so you cross the top of any climb fast, and then you can make best use of any descent that follows.

Feeding

In longer events, if you want to feed, make sure you start doing it before you need to, taking a little food or food-drink every ten miles or so. Choose moments when the course or wind direction make the going fast, so that the act of taking one hand off the bars won't make you lose too much speed.

When you are feeding, try not to gulp down air with the food. It will ruin your digestion. Drinking is made easier by using feeding bottles with caps which allow you to squirt a controlled jet into your mouth by just squeezing the sides.

The longer the event, incidentally, the less willing will your stomach be to accept solid food in the later stages. So the best idea is to count on your main food coming in liquid form, and keep some solid food just to keep your palate interested. Try this liquid food beforehand – on long training rides, for instance.

Schedules

Some riders are best blasting their way around the course with no regard to what time they might be doing. Others get pathological about whether or not they are doing well.

In short events, carrying a stopwatch is of dubious value, since the loss of concentration as you look at the watch and try to interpret its verdict will lose you time. It can be of some use, however, if you know the course and where various intermediate distances are – because then at least you can compare your progress with your target time.

In longer events, especially those of more than 50 miles, you will probably draw up a schedule anyway, to help find the right pace. You should have two schedules ready for use depending on the wind direction. Early gains on a schedule for a hard start and a fast finish are only significant if these gains are made into a head wind.

You can tape this schedule on to the top of your handlebar stem, and monitor your progress. But don't let it do any more than act as a rough guide to your progress. It is not unknown for a rider to give up because he was badly down on his schedule, only to find that he was leading the event at the time, and had simply not made the mental adjustment for the tough conditions.

In conclusion

Time trials are a special kind of event which calls for an unusual amount of concentration and commitment. After all, in road racing one of the considerations is to save energy, while in time trialling the challenge is to expend energy at such a rate that you reach exhaustion point as you pass the finish timekeeper. In short, you have to hurt yourself all the way round.

However, punishing your muscles by application of your mind to the task is *not* something you can do well if you try to do it frequently. Britain's top time triallists have frequently gone abroad to meet other Europeans in time trials and have come home badly beaten. Such races have often been at the end of a long season during which, for week after week, they had been forcing both body and mind to make a supreme effort. The effect was that they were jaded. On the other hand, their European rivals, being more used to road racing, were mentally fresh to the challenge of the time trial; and with a little special preparation and a special bike, they had the motivation that the British TT champions lacked.

Paradoxically, then, it seems that the aspiring time triallist should ride fewer time trials as he moves closer to the top. Having learned the techniques of the unpaced game, he now has to sharpen his motivation for the big occasions. This can be done by interspersing them with road races – criteriums (short-circuit races) being very good for building speed – and track races, which promote fluid pedalling as well as speed.

Alternatively, if you don't choose to road-race or be a track rider, then you must consciously ride some of your time trials for fun and for training: experiment with different techniques and gearing, but save the real mental effort for the days when the titles are at stake, or the conditions are right for fast times.

Team time trials

This event is for roadmen used to working hard, rather than for individual time triallists. The rhythm, with efforts interspersed with recovery periods, is more akin to a road-race breakaway than a time trial. Most time triallists find the speed of their efforts at the front too high, and are upset by the changes in pace.

Good time-trial teams are equally balanced in fitness and build. They should be drawn from the ranks of the mature pursuiters and criterium riders, and coached in the techniques of combining their efforts with others.

Team time trialling in the Tour de France style. With quite a number of riders in the team, the event is like a well-drilled road-race breakaway.

Team time trialling in the 1983 world championships. There are four riders per team, and the distance of 100 kilometres is covered in about two hours. These are the East Germans, who have regularly won at world and Olympic level. Note the similar physiques of the team members, and the superb formation riding.

The Great Britain team in the same event (left). They use aerodynamic helmets, but the road bikes are standard. Contrast them with the East German machines.

4 *Cyclo-cross*

Cyclo-cross started off as a fun sport used mainly as a way of keeping fit during the winter. Most cyclo-cross riders now specialise, and use the spring and summer to build themselves up for September and the start of their season.

It still is fun, of course, and the different courses mix large quantities of the unpredictable into every race recipe. To be a good cyclo-cross rider you need the qualities of a roadman, plus a runner's legs and the daring of a trapeze artist.

The cyclo-cross machine

Cyclo-cross uses a modified road-racing machine, the main modification being a longer frame (for a 'smoother' ride) and massive clearances around the wheels to stop the frame being fouled by a build-up of mud.

For the same reason, conventional side-pull brakes are rejected in favour of brazed-on cantilever brakes which are light, powerful, and virtually impossible to clog with mud.

Much of cyclo-cross racing calls for the skill and stamina of a runner, with the bike carried over the shoulder.

Lower gears are used, of course, since the going is rarely fast; but a 14-tooth top sprocket is quite common, to take care of any road sections, while a bottom sprocket of 28 teeth is the favourite. This is coupled with a moderate chainwheel of perhaps 45 teeth, with a chainguard outside it to stop the chain derailing. Sometimes double chainwheels are used, and in that case the front changer serves a similar purpose to the chainguard.

Because it is important to keep both hands on the handlebars for as long as possible, the normal down-tube gear levers are replaced by levers plugged into the ends of the handlebars.

The pedals are wide and double-sided, and special double toe-clips are used because single clips are liable to break when a big cyclo-cross boot lands on top of them by mistake.

Small-flange hubs are the norm, generally with 36 spokes; but the top riders occasionally gamble on lighter wheels. The wheels are shod with special knobbly tyres: the more mud, the more pronounced the knobbles.

Position

This is very similar to road racing, except that the saddle might be a touch lower and the bars slightly higher.

Clothing

Cyclo-cross spans a season of varying weather, so this will determine the garb. Skinsuits are used over other jerseys in cold

The cyclo-cross machine must be capable of being ridden up steep muddy slopes. Note the special cantilever brakes for good wheel clearance, and the gear levers at the ends of the handlebars.

weather, and the road jerseys are also preferred for their natural feel. Some special cyclo-cross jerseys have a pad on the shoulder where the bike is carried.

The other special requirement concerns the shoes: some riders use trainers, but most specialists now go for a medium-cut bootee with removable studs on the heel and a ribbed sole, offering two kinds of grip, plus ankle support at the same time.

Techniques

Cyclo-cross varies tremendously in its courses, from the mainly rideable, to the slogging courses where there is more 'cross' than 'cyclo'. But since even the riding is far from fast, and because of the mud and grassland involved, the main requirement is strength. Devotees of this sport need strong shoulders and arms to keep the bike on their shoulder effortlessly when required, and to hold the bike in check over rough ground.

Running must also figure in the training programme, because it most certainly figures in the racing. And since you must run with your bike shouldered, the majority of the running training should be this way too.

Races are partly anaerobic – and this is where the fit rider scores. Running with a bike up near-vertical mud banks can be a destroyer of the less fit. The man who can hang on to run over the top will open vast gaps in front of rivals who reach their anaerobic thresholds more quickly. And there is no respite on descents either, for these can be as testing as the ascents.

It is particularly important to get a good start, and a hard warm-up is

Don't automatically follow the tracks of the rider in front. The average 'cross course allows you to take an alternative line in most cases, which you should have worked out during pre-event reconnoitring of the course. Watch for good, firmer alternatives to muddy patches, which will get muddier as the event progresses. Similarly, look for firm ground on the climbs, both on and off the bike. If you have found a good alternative line which no one else seems to be using, then keep it up your sleeve until later in the event, when it might be just the key to gaining a place or two once the field has settled down into its rough finishing order – as it tends to do around half-distance.

Use the saddle as a stabilising point on rough descents; but when the going gets really rough and a daunting obstacle approaches, you should stand on the pedals, and at the very last moment heave upwards on bars and pedals and try to hop your bike over it. Practice makes perfect here.

Make no mistake: cyclo-cross demands great fitness; and this can make it a useful winter pursuit for road riders wanting to develop their strength and to keep the competitive edge. It has also contributed several of its stars to the road game, among them Roger De Vlaeminck of Belgium, Germany's Rolf Wolfshohl, and Britain's Chris Wreghitt.

An uphill run on a muddy slope can be a destroyer of the unfit.

necessary to open up your lungs in time for the first sprint away from the flag. Because of the inevitable bottlenecks on the course, you cannot afford to take your time to work your way up through the field. Make a slow start and you can often be brought to a dead halt on narrow sections, baulked by lesser riders who got a better start.

5 *Track racing*

When a rider decides to race on the track he commits himself to an event where success and failure come under the same spotlights. At its best, track racing is spectacular, thrilling and super-fast. At worst, it is – for the spectators at least – lack-lustre.

Who could fail to have been brought to their feet by Reg Harris in the 1950s, sprinting home at speeds that were rarely equalled a decade later? – or by the bitter battle over the final hour of a six-day race, when teams take lap after lap in an attempt to gain ground over the opposition? – or by the sight of Hugh Porter in the 1970s, showing the world that a slow start in a long pursuit does not mean a title lost?

Most trackmen are all-rounders these days, since specialisation has gone by the board with, sadly, the fall in popularity of track meetings. Only the internationals specialise to any degree, and of those only the sprinters are true specialists.

This means that track racing is wide open to any road cyclist who is ready to try his luck. He will certainly benefit from track racing in terms of increased speed on the road, and might possibly find that he really takes to track racing. If you have a road racer's fitness sharpened by criterium racing, you will be able to handle most bunched

The thrills and spills of track sprinting. In the 1982 world championship final at Leicester, Japan's Nakano crosses the line while Canada's Singleton is decked.

events on the track and put up a good showing in pursuiting. Only the true sprint events are likely to demand specialist training.

The track bike

Although track bikes are lighter than road bikes because they have no brakes and variable gears, they are not specially built for lightness. In fact, a bike for a burly sprinter will be built for strength, with sturdy seat and chain stays.

Track frames have steep angles, straight or almost straight forks, and high bottom-bracket clearances to cater for banked tracks.

Track bikes. Note the sturdy front forks, the large-flange hubs, the sloping handlebar stems and the deep handlebars.

virtually any length because they do not use the banking.

Handlebars are deeper and less square than on the road, sloping stems being normal for track racing; steeply-sloping stems are used to give the low handlebar position necessary for sprinting.

A different kind of machine is used for the high speeds of

The urgent pursuiting position of 1983 world amateur champion Viktor Koupovets of the Soviet Union. The shoes are fixed to the pedals to obviate the use of toe-clips; the handlebars are of an aerodynamic design, as is the racing helmet. The skinsuit is plasticised for better airflow. Note once again how the rider has moved forward on his saddle so that he can use his thigh strength on a big gear.

motor-paced racing. This has a 24-inch front wheel, a much bigger chainwheel, and special supports for the saddle peak and handlebar stem because of the stresses on them at racing speeds. The tyres are held on to the rims using a special bandaging technique below the tread, because a roll-off at speed could easily be fatal; for the same reason special crash-hats with extra protection are used.

Position

Six-day riders stay comfortable and use a road position. Pursuiters lift the saddle height slightly – while sprinters have the most extreme position, with legs fully straightened when the crank is at its lowest point, the saddle further forward than on the road, and bars so deep that the rider's arms are straight virtually all the time.

The wheels are sturdy for sprinters, lighter for pursuiters. Almost all have large-flange hubs, with spoking according to events. Sprinters have 36 spokes, often tied and soldered where they cross. Pursuiters are happy with 36, 32, or often 28, since this event is nowhere near so punishing.

Transmission is by a single fixed gear, using a chain width of either ⅛-inch or ³⁄₃₂, the latter being increasingly popular. The single chainring should be easy to change; part of the tactics of track racing is to have just the right gear for your physique and the conditions.

Cranks tend to be shorter than the 170mm which is normal for roads; 165mm is needed for any manoeuvring on steeply-banked tracks – though pursuiters can use

Clothing

Trackmen are natural posers. They haven't to contend with the extremes of climate that roadmen suffer, and generally race in the warmest weather. So they cultivate good-looking gear. Trackies were using silk shorts years before skinshorts were thought of, matching them with silk vests to optimise aerodynamics.

Trackmen started the move towards skinsuits – and the study of aerodynamics in general – because on the track the speeds are higher, and the wind is less of a factor thanks to the natural protection of the banking; so it is worth experimenting for the sake of a split-second advantage.

Cold is the enemy at track meets, where riders are often marooned in the track centre between events. If you start track racing, develop the habit of changing racing vests frequently, together with the woollen undervest which is a permanent 'must'. If you wear two racing vests over the undervest, this will minimise crash injuries as the top jersey will slide against the one underneath it. Wear a tracksuit to warm up in, and have a good heavy coat to wear in the track centre between events.

Shoes should be close-fitting (socks are not normally worn), and track mitts and crash hats should be substantial in case of crashes.

Skinsuits are taking over as standard trackwear – but not so much in six-day and Madison racing (see page 68), where the long time spent in the saddle means that you'll welcome the extra comfort of woollen shorts. In Madison racing, extra padding on the hip is needed for the change-over. The saddle

Six-day racing style: substantial track mitts, varnished crash hat and silky track vest. This is Holland's Joop Zoetemelk, better known as a road rider.

area takes a real pounding through the distance and the fast pedalling, so pay particular attention to the quality of the chamois insert in your shorts, and keep it clean and well lubricated.

Sprint racing

Sprinters are the greyhounds of the track, combining strength, speed and skill.

It is not sufficient for a sprinter to be the fastest man on the track. He must also have the tactical skill to outwit his rivals, and the daring to go for an opening during the split second that it is available. Sprinters are men of decision – aggressive and volatile. They are the most specialised of cyclists, in that they

are suited for very little else on track or road.

The classic sprinter has powerful thighs, and keeps them that way by regular weight training even during the height of the season. He needs to have a strong upper body as well as strong legs, because the arms and shoulders are brought into play during the accelerations which are the key to sprinting.

Sprinting is not just a matter of blasting away from the gun and going flat out for the finish. Because of the slipstreaming effect, any rival would counter that tactic by 'sitting in' until the final straight and simply cruising by, having saved his energies for just that moment.

It is a game of cat and mouse. The lead man is at a disadvantage, so tries to trick or otherwise persuade the man or men behind to trade positions.

Hence the standstill tactics which are frequently seen in match sprinting. There is a rule that the lead-off man must keep rolling for the first lap. By suddenly slowing up, he might surprise his rival into going past him – but this is unlikely. So, after the compulsory first lap, the lead rider comes to a halt, turns his handlebars and rocks almost imperceptibly backward and forward using his fixed wheel.

Experienced riders can stand still this way for many minutes, but it is wearing on the legs and the brain. The flexed thighs begin to stiffen up; doubt begins to creep in as to whether this was a good idea; the mind strays – and suddenly the other rider explodes into full sprint and heads for home. In practice such a tactic is rarely used. Eventually one or other sprinter rolls gently forward and the standstill is over until the next time.

The classic track sprinter has large and powerful legs thanks to power weight training, and well-muscled shoulders and arms to augment the leg-power.

The shorter the track, the less important the sheltered position will be, because the finishing straight will be shorter, leaving less opportunity for the sheltered rider to jump past.

The real sprint tends to wind up around the 200-metre mark, when one rider or the other will make his move. This can happen in a variety of ways; here are some of them.

1. The lead rider keeps high on the banking, goes as slow as he dares, and slows right up as he enters the back straight. The following rider, still on the banking, cannot slow up suddenly and either faces a fall and a slide down the track on his hip, or attacks by jumping for the inside. The lead rider anticipates this tactic and counters it by dropping down the track to block the attack, then sprinting away to win.

Women sprinters try a track standstill. The riders are virtually stationary, but in fact are rocking slightly backwards and forwards using their fixed gear, with the handlebars turned to give increased stability.

2. The lead rider tries the same tactic, but the following rider anticipates it and attacks as he sees the leader start to slow. He is through the gap and away to win.

3. The lead rider enters the back straight five metres up the track, offering the following rider room to pass either outside or inside. He spots a move in either direction, moves to block it, and sprints away to win.

4. The lead rider tempts the following rider to try passing on the outside, then moves up to pin him against the outer fence. The follower must ease back, which leaves the leader the necessary advantage to win.

5. The lead rider tries tactic 3, but the following rider stays on his wheel. Once past the 200-metre mark, the leader must stay in roughly the same line; so the contest is one of pure speed, the second rider having the advantage of the slipstream. In such circumstances, the leader should minimise this advantage by delaying the onset of the sprint as long as possible.

6. The lead rider tries tactic 3, upon which the second rider switches up to the outer fence, threatening to use the banking to dive inside the leader. He tries this halfway round the last banking, his extra speed down the banking bringing him inside the leader before he can 'shut the door'. It is important to hang back just far enough (this is called 'laying off') so that the leader finds it difficult to see you because you are in his 'blind spot'.

Sprinting used to be a very physical game, in which bumping shoulders and clashing pedals were quite the norm. More recently, international judges have tended to frown on rough-house tactics, so speed has become more and more of the essence. The fabulous Japanese Koichi Nakano, who has won more world pro sprint titles than any other, based his early wins on superior speed, and only subsequently developed tactics to match. It is a sobering thought that if

Track sprinting used to be a contact sport, but judges now discourage this kind of tactic.

The fastest man in the world for nearly a decade, Japan's Koichi Nakano (nearest camera), holds off Yave Cahard of France.

you can go half a second faster than your opponent over the last 200 metres, you can afford to make quite a lot of tactical errors.

There is no such thing as a standard track, and this is where track craft comes in. A sprinter should know every inch of the track: its quirky transitions, the slippery nature of the advertising paint on the track surface, the flat bit at the top of the track where the track builder didn't get it right, the bump coming out of the final bend – all these can be turned to advantage.

The sprinter must be at one with his machine, and know exactly how he needs to distribute his weight so that the back wheel doesn't hop about when he accelerates out of the saddle.

He must be able to time his last-metre lunge to gain a little at the end. He must be cool enough to ride slowly at the top of a steep banking, or to carry on flat-out on the final bend with another rider at his hip.

Most of all, he must be able to plan and re-plan his tactics, to recognise his opponents' strengths and weaknesses, and to revise his tactics accordingly in an instant. If he is master of a long sprint, he must engineer the race to provide one. If he is best at short sprints, then he must keep stalling so that the sprint starts late, or – knowing that his opponent will expect him to stall – do exactly the opposite.

He must cultivate, above all, the explosive effort from zero to maximum speed in a handful of seconds – sheer power into sheer speed in a twinkling. Speed can be cultivated by training with a Derny pacing motor-bike.

If you fancy yourself as a future sprinter, then go and watch as much top-class sprinting as you can, until you know exactly why every race has been won and lost. Then go out and try to win some yourself.

For the intrepid, there is tandem sprinting too, which uses many of the same tactics at a higher speed. Standstills are trickier and therefore rare, and the wind-up usually starts much earlier. Otherwise the principles are the same – only the stakes are doubled.

Handicap racing

This is the younger brother of sprinting. Riders go flat-out from a standing start for a given distance. There are a good few riders on the track, and their starting positions are separated according to ability by the handicapper. The best man starts with a handicap, the worst with a good start. In theory, they should all cross the line together. In practice, the slower riders have the advantage since they are usually improving, while the 'scratchman' will only rarely come up to his previous best. This is fine training for sprinting, although without the tactics.

Kilometre time trials

This is a track time trial for the sprinter. Riders have a held start, and cover the kilometre as fast as they can. The successful kilometre man will have a high anaerobic threshold and the ability to drive himself around the final lap, which is the graveyard of the faint-hearted. Top kilometre riders have come unstuck by starting too fast and 'dying' over the final 200 metres.

Tandem sprinting.

Top sprinters are usually the best kilometre riders by virtue of their speed potential; but the heavier sprinters are now losing out to the leaner ones, who may not have so much explosive power but can hold their effort longer. Key to the 'kilo' is speed, and training should aim first to attain the speed and then gradually prolong the distance. Some time also needs to be spent on the technique of starting, which can gain valuable time.

Pursuiting

Pursuiting is when two riders start from opposite sides of the track and chase one another round for a given distance, or until one rider catches up with the other.

Over the years, British riders have excelled in pursuiting. In the beginning it was because there were thousands of enthusiastic time triallists raised on racing on a fixed wheel, who were therefore ideal pursuiting material. More recently, fast-pedalling roadmen have made the transition into pursuiting, and it is still easy for roadmen to sharpen up for pursuiting with a little track training.

Over the past decade, pursuiting speeds have taken a great leap forward, to the extent that the 4000-metre pursuit (the amateur world championship distance) has needed almost the speed of the sprinter. This could be seen happening earlier in team pursuits, where talented sprinters not quite at top level found a natural home in the team-pursuit event.

Pursuiting calls for speed and stamina; it suits a fast pedaller, and a rider with a cool head. Often,

pursuits have been won and lost by means of bluff: one rider has started so fast that he has broken the spirit of his opponent. The counter tactic against a known fast starter is to aim to match his starting effort, then ease slightly, and pile on the

The professional pursuiting style of Frenchman Alain Bondue.

pressure when he in turn has to ease.

If neither rider is prone to bluff or tactics, it comes to a straightforward test of speed and judgement. Part of a pursuit tournament is the homework done on the track – finding out its speed potential so that a schedule can be prepared. If you are lucky enough to ride late in a series of pursuit qualifying rounds, then note down the lap times of your main rivals and decide your schedules accordingly. You will need a trackside helper when you ride, to let you know by pre-arranged signals how you stand in relation to your schedule and to your direct opponent.

Pursuit tournaments start with a qualifying round, usually with one man on the track at a time; the best eight or sixteen riders will qualify. These are then matched fastest against slowest, second fastest against second slowest, and so on, all through the rounds until two finalists are obtained. Thus the aim is not just to beat your opponent, but to beat him in as fast a time as possible, so as to give yourself the best chance in the next round. You can only take an easy win in the semi-final if you know that you are the fastest man on the track – and you're right about it!

Once again, the emphasis in pursuit training must be on speed. The only techniques are those of starting correctly and being able to follow a good line on the inside of the track. Roadmen will always have the stamina for pursuiting, but will need to train over shorter distances and hence higher speeds to get the necessary velocity.

Team pursuiting

Team pursuiting is an exciting development of pursuiting, in which four-man teams ride a match, starting each side of the track as in standard pursuiting. The time for

Team pursuiting. The East German team seem almost to be riding a single eight-wheeled machine, so tight is their formation.

each team is taken from the third man to cross the line; so each quartet must concentrate above all on staying together, until the last lap, when one man can put in his final burst and peel off.

Riders share the pace, say, on an average track, by doing half a lap at the front, then peeling off as they enter the banking, and swooping up to the top and down again to join the tail of the string. This is a precision matter, and can be disastrous if mistimed. Occasionally riders find the pace too hard and a gap opens. It is then a matter of quick adjustment to close the gap and nurse the weaker rider until he is no longer needed. There have been many good team-pursuit squads over the years, bred out of true team commitment. The most successful ones were foursomes who spent most of the season racing together, and who raced for the team rather than personal glory.

One memorable day in 1973, the Great Britain team of Mick Bennett, Ian Hallam, Willi Moore and Rick Evans reached the final of the world championship in San Sebastian, Spain. With half a lap to go, the Britons were well beaten; then came a fearful crash and their West German opponents were spread all over the track. Someone had touched a wheel and the Germans did not finish.

Technically, the British quartet were world champions. In fact, they refused to accept the medals. Such was the spirit of a team that respected the true status of the event rather than its technical outcome. No British team since has ever approached the achievements of that team.

Points races

This is now a world championship event, in which a bunch races for points for each nominated lap; it is the overall points winner, not the first man across the line at the end, who takes the gold. This is an ideal event for a roadman-pursuiter because of the combination of speed, skill and stamina demanded.

Devil

Hardly a speed event, but definitely one of skill. The last rider across the line is eliminated in each nominated lap, until the sprint for the line. A fun event and good training.

Keirin

A recent addition to the world championship timetable, this event was conceived in Japan, where it is practised most of all. A nominated pacemaker (on a small motorcycle in the world event) drags behind him the string of competing riders, who may jockey for positions but not pass the leader until the bell lap. For sprinters and tough guys!

Motor-paced racing

This is a code apart. Riders race behind large pacing motorcycles at speeds of around 80kph. The techniques of the event revolve around choosing the moment to make an attacking move, since passing a rider means fighting your way through the buffeting of his motorcycle's slipstream. If you

cannot pass quickly and cleanly, you will use up too much strength. To counter a passing effort, the leading rider (or in fact his pacer, since they are as much the tacticians) will accelerate so that the attacker is forced off his own pacing motor by the wind of the slipstream. Events last for about an hour, and when fields are well balanced, many laps are spent in working up to the right moment for an attack.

Madison racing

Madisons were popularised in New York's Madison Square Garden and are still most popular as the corner-stone of indoor six-day racing.

Six-day events and Madisons are contested by teams of two riders, who continuously relay one another around the track, one racing while his partner takes a breather. They change by touch, either by a shove in the seat of the pants or by the racing rider grabbing the other's hand and throwing him into action. The length of each relay is optional.

Madison racing is a matter of gaining a full lap on your nearest rivals by the finish. If teams are equal on laps, then the winners are the team with the most intermediate sprint points.

Road criterium riders with track skill are ideal for this event. It

In the closing metres of a finishing sprint, the roadman-sprinter can open impressive gaps on those rivals he was shadowing just seconds before. John Herety makes the point in winning the 1982 British professional road championship.

Above left: The first instant of a kilometre time trial effort. Note how the muscles of the upper arms are brought into action.

Above right: Top British time triallist Ian Cammish on the type of aerodynamic time-trial machine found more and more frequently. It is not designed to do any tight cornering, or to tackle rough roads

Left: Oersted of Denmark, on his way to the 1984 world pro pursuit championship. Aerodynamic touches to the machine are a small front wheel, a disc-type rear wheel and shortened handlebars. His clothing includes overshoes, crash-hat and skinsuit, all designed for better airflow.

Right: Interval training demands immense commitment from the rider, and a high-quality effort over short period.

requires immense stamina and the ability to recover quickly. Small, tightly-banked indoor tracks pose problems of 'seasickness' for inexperienced riders unable to settle to the idea of lapping every ten seconds or so, coupled with the challenge of finding your partner in a melée of so many other riders.

As in road racing, the essence of good Madison riding is the correct judgement of the time when your attack is likely to find the others unwilling to react. This enables laps to be taken quickly and with the least expenditure of energy.

The confused appearance of a Madison race, in which only half the field is racing at one time; the other half rest by riding more slowly on the upper part of the track.

The Madison changeover, modern-style. The right-hand rider, Aussie Don Allan, has just handed over to his compatriot partner Danny Clark. Clark is launching himself forward using Allan as a resistance. The other changeover method is when the relieved rider grabs his partner by the seat of the pants and slings him into action.

Left: Bob Downs makes another gut-wrenching effort during a pro criterium. Such repeated efforts would not be possible without plenty of high-intensity work in training.

6 Race routine

Whatever the event, you should follow a planned preparation routine beforehand and an equally planned post-race routine to start your recovery.

Pre-race preparation starts the day before the event, when you check your equipment and pack your race bag.

The important meal is dinner on the eve of the race. You are looking for energy, so steer clear of foods like salads that have low energy content but will bulk you up. The best energy-producing foods are carbohydrates, so this meal should have plenty of potatoes, pasta or bread. The meal should be substantial, and should therefore not be taken too close to bedtime. If you go to bed straight after this big meal you will have disturbed sleep.

Next morning, if you are riding a short-distance time trial or road race, the breakfast is not all that important. You only need something to take up the acids in your stomach and satisfy your hunger – perhaps some toast and honey or some muesli, but nothing too heavy. Don't have steak and salad or steak and rice before an early event. It will just weigh you down.

If, however, your event is later during the day, and you have to travel to the race, then you need a good breakfast of mixed protein and carbohydrate. In this case steak and and rice or pasta would be acceptable, but so would the traditional breakfast. Just avoid highly spiced, fatty or sickening foods.

Travel to the race in comfort and allow plenty of time. Anything that goes wrong usually happens on the way to the race. Plan to arrive at least an hour before the start. Find the changing-rooms and toilets, and start to sort yourself out. Go through your personal preparation and don your racing gear. Massage your legs and apply your embrocations according to the weather. Immediately after using embrocation, wipe your hands with cologne to remove all traces.

As you take off your everyday clothes and don your racing gear, make sure that you pack the discarded clothes into your race bag, which should be marked with your name. This is in the interests of the safety of your belongings, and also so that your belongings can easily be gathered up and sent on to you if you crash and are sent to hospital. Incidentally, don't take lots of money with you. Any valuables should be left with a race official, and not in the changing-rooms.

Don socks and shoes, have a drink if you wish, and have your bike checked; then sign on in good time and go for a warm-up. Wear a tracksuit to ensure that you are warm during this period.

At the start of the race, pass your tracksuit to a helper, and you're

Scotsman Robert Millar personally checks his bike before a race start.

Race requirements

It is surprising how many items you can suddenly need out at a race, and sometimes disastrous when you don't have them to hand. So let's draw on the experience of Bob Downs – a Great Britain international amateur and later a professional – and see what he puts in his race bag.

Single-day events:

Tool bag with spare parts, including a spare gear and brake cable
Spare tyres of good racing quality
Towel and soap
Shampoo
Small bottle of cologne and a flannel – particularly useful for cleaning your hands after applying embrocation or massage cream
Embrocations for all types of weather
Pair of nail clippers
Spare shoelaces
Shoe-cleaning kit
Shoe-plates and spanner
Hairbrush
Chamois cream
Wet-weather gear: overshoes, oversocks, gloves, cotton caps, nylon cap, racing cape, nylon bib, thermal underwear (Damart is good)
Racing licence and proof of any anti-tetanus injections
Racing clothes:
Crash hat
Track mitts
2 pairs of white socks
2 pairs of shoes
Racing cap
Racing shorts
Racing jerseys
Arm-warmers
Undervests and bib

Stage races:

Spare parts: chainrings, sprockets and spare tyres. (Even if you are going with a national team you shouldn't count on the team mechanic having spares for your particular machine)
Towels
Soap
Shampoo
Hair dryer
Razor (with international adaptor if electric)
Washbag
Embrocation bag with your preferred embrocations (because the soigneur may not have enough of the one you like)
Nail clippers
Shoelaces
Shoe-cleaning kit
Shoe-plates and spanner
Hairbrush
Chamois cream
Wet weather clothes as for single-day events
Racing licence and proof of any anti-tetanus injections

Racing clothes as for single-day events, except:
Spare crash hat, because crash hats tend to be 'lifted' as souvenirs by spectators. (Develop the habit of putting it straight into your back pocket immediately after the stage finish)
Plenty of track mitts and socks according to the length of the race
At least 2 pairs of racing shoes
8 cotton racing caps, always keeping a dry one for after the finish
8 pairs of racing shorts (laundry service is not always reliable)
4 racing jerseys
5 undervests
2 bibs

Have a bag marked with your name and possibly also your race number: pack it with warm clothes and washing materials for after the finish. Include a tracksuit and a hat.

away, hopefully, for your best ride ever.

After the race is over – and let's assume you've done a good ride and are among the first to finish – you should get cleaned up for the prize presentation. Your helper should be at the finish with a drink, a cologne wash, and a flannel to wipe your face. Don a tracksuit and a clean race hat for the presentation.

Even if you haven't won a prize, go through the same routine, but then go to the showers as quickly as possible. Do not stand around waiting to catch a chill.

You will want to take off your tight racing shoes, but don't then go padding around in bare feet, at the mercy of grit and powdered glass. Have a pair of slip-on sandals ready in your bag, to help protect and relax your feet.

Make your way to the showers; clean off the embrocation with cologne or soap, and rinse it off well afterwards. Don clean, warm clothing; and have a drink and relax before the journey home.

Frank Westell waiting at a race finish for his team to arrive. Each rider has his own race bag waiting by the team vehicle, with warm clothes and washing gear.

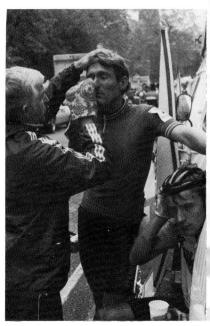

Westell uses a flannel glove with sport cologne to wipe away the grime on the face of one of his team, while another sips a post-race drink.

7 Training

Fitness has a 'family tree'

When you start to turn the pedals in search of success, you may think that all you need is a high degree of fitness. But the route to success is much more complex than that.

Your training needs to be carefully planned in all aspects. As you start racing and begin to build towards a peak, it is important to realise that physical fitness is not the only area in which you must progress. Quite apart from specific training in cycling and racing skills, there are other factors to be taken into consideration, without which your success will be limited. The equipment must be right: the bike and your clothing. And your mind must be right, so that you can make best use of the physical fitness you have attained.

The chart shows just how many factors must be worked upon if you are to stand the best chance of success. As you work towards your goal, keeping looking back at the chart to check that you are moving forward on all fronts.

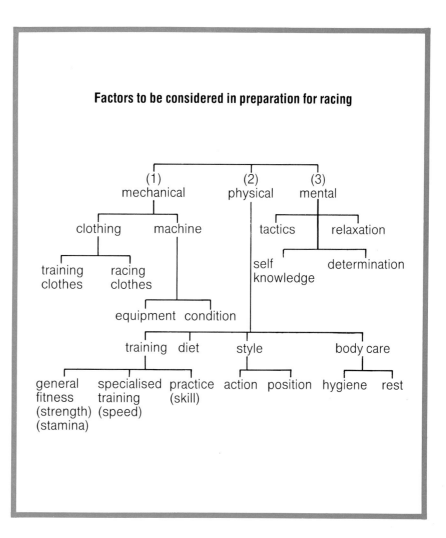

Factors to be considered in preparation for racing

The training cocktail

For many cyclists the Sunday club run, coupled with their racing, constitutes all of their training. Others ride three times a week around the same circuit – nice and steady, or perhaps flat-out – but always following the same style. But it is only by varying your training that you can get the best out of yourself, because different types of training benefit your body in different ways. A sort of training cocktail, where the result of the mixture is more than any of its ingredients.

Muscle types

Take a look at a muscle under a microscope and you will see that it is composed of red fibres and white fibres. The red fibres are called 'slow-twitch' fibres and the white fibres are called 'fast-twitch' fibres. The red fibres have the quality of being able to stand constant repetition work, and as such are good for work requiring stamina. White fibres are capable of fast work, but only for a comparatively short period of time.

We all have different proportions of slow- and fast-twitch fibres, and it is generally accepted that we never actually change the proportions. However, training will develop them in different ways.

If you continue to train using the slow-twitch fibres, you will improve them, but do very little to improve the fast-twitch fibres – and vice versa. So you must work to improve

both types; and bear in mind that, because the essence of cycle racing is speed, you must pay heed to developing the fast-twitch fibres in particular. You can only do this by going fast. This is why training should start with steady-state rides to develop local muscular endurance and stamina, and should then include fast work to improve your speed.

Consider this in relation to the development of the heart chamber and its surrounding muscle (see page 84) and you will appreciate

Russia's Sergei Kopylov – sprinter supreme. His speed comes from the preponderance of fast-twitch white fibres in his muscles.

how a training plan is built up. If you only train at steady state (less than 150 pulse beats per minute), then you will enlarge the heart chamber and improve your stamina but with no increase in speed. If you concentrate on anaerobic work (taking the pulse rate over 150) then you will increase the muscle wall of the heart without greatly increasing its capacity. You will be able to go fast, but only very briefly.

The ideal course is to start with aerobic work, and then blend in anaerobic work once the chamber has been enlarged. The result is a strong, slow pulse with plenty of blood pumped around at each beat. So the ideal heart is achieved by the same training mix which is also best for your muscles.

It is essential to mix your training

with the aim of improving the four S's of speed, strength, skill and stamina. Here are the basic types of training which should be found in a balanced plan:

LSD (long, steady, distance)

This is the cornerstone of training. This basic aerobic training, building up stamina, will develop all the body systems. It is measured in hours spent in the saddle, the eventual duration depending on the amount of time normally spent racing. The farther you expect to race, the longer the LSD sessions should become. Although important as a basis for a programme, it isn't a very efficient investment in time. LSD can be done alone or in a group. Company is an advantage, because conversation helps to relieve the soul-destroying monotony. The duration can start at half an hour if you are a real beginner, and go up to the high levels of professional and international amateur riders, who might be in the saddle for as long as six hours. Gears should be medium, allowing you to pedal at optimum revs but comfortably, and to keep up a steady effort. The duration of sessions should gradually be extended, and as time goes on not only does the distance increase, but so also does the speed because of increased fitness.

Basic speed or paced-effort training

This is the next level of aerobic training, in which you cut down the distance involved but concentrate on going faster, pacing your effort throughout. This is still aerobic work, but with the emphasis on improving speed. For instance, a would-be 25-mile time triallist would move from LSD work into riding 25 miles at a constant pace throughout, gauging his effort not only to last the distance, but also to extend himself in doing so. Nearer the start of the season, he would cut down the distance in order to increase his speed – since it is clearly not possible to train at full race speed over the full race distance because there is not sufficient motivation. Training feels quite different from racing: you are wearing different clothing, you are on heavier tyres, and you miss the spectators and the race atmosphere.

Remember that if you want to go fast over a given distance, you must first attain that speed over a shorter distance. This type of training will develop speed, and will also accustom your muscles to work at reasonable levels of lactic acid content.* The constant pressure of this training will enable you to start racing during this period.

Bit-and-bit

This is a mixture of aerobic and anaerobic work. You go out in company, in a group of six for preference, which will give you

*Lactic acid is the substance that is deposited within your muscles when you extend yourself, and which produces much of the pain of effort.

Lactic acid hurts. This waste product of energy release builds up during anaerobic effort, producing the classic pain in muscles which have been used to the limit.

enough of a recovery period in between efforts at the front. You ride in single file, changing the lead every 100 to 200 metres, the front rider making an effort which will produce a build-up of lactic acid within the muscles. The time taken to ease to the back of the string and gradually move up to the front again should be long enough to allow this lactic acid to be dispersed. Bit-and-bit enables you to develop speed and endurance, because it combines efforts involving both the slow-twitch and the fast-twitch fibres. This type of training is very similar to the kind of regular effort you will make in road racing when working in a bunch or in a breakaway, so you should gear up almost to racing levels.

Interval training

This is a system of planned efforts and rest periods. In fact, the rest periods should be long enough to allow only partial recovery – that is, to allow the pulse rate to come down from 150–180 beats per minute to 120–130.

Efforts should be flat-out for their duration, and similarly rest periods should be of very easy riding, just turning the pedals over.

Interval training is subdivided into short, medium or long intervals, depending on the type of racing effort which is required. If you are going in for a more intensive type of speed training, your efforts will be short, and so will your periods of rest.

Short-interval training has effort periods of between 15 seconds and one minute. During this time you are working anaerobically.

Medium-interval training has efforts of between 3 and 10 minutes. This is the sort of training you would employ in speed-stamina work for short-distance road races or time trials. You cannot work anaerobically for effort periods this long, but your pulse rate is gradually pushed up and up by very hard work until it reaches about 180 beats per minute, coming down to 130 or so during the rest period.

Long-interval training efforts vary from 10 to 15 minutes, and are suitable training for longer road races or distance time trials.

Interval training works both aerobically and anaerobically, and during the effort periods you should use gears either at or just below those used when racing.

It is extremely tough training and

consequently will be of shorter duration than a steady-state outing. The emphasis should be on quality rather than quantity, and you should begin the new effort only when the desired recovery pulse rate has been achieved. With practice you can adjust your goals in interval training, gradually lengthening the efforts and decreasing the rest periods to achieve progression.

Fartlek

Once you have reached a high level of training, you sometimes need to ease off for a session – and this is where fartlek or 'speed play' comes into its own. This is a kind of mock racing – going out in a group, working steadily but well within your capacity, occasionally sprinting for a given point on the road. These short periods of effort with plenty of time to recover ensure that your level of fitness is maintained by means of an enjoyable form of training in company.

On-the-bike strength training

This type of training should be carried out using medium-high gears. The aim is to go from a slow speed to a maximum in as short a time as possible, and then ease again; the quality of the training depends on your being able to pour in maximum effort over this very short period. For this reason, such efforts should be made at evenly-spaced intervals during a steady training ride, but not at the end, when you would be too tired to produce a quality effort. This is

good for developing strength and power, and will improve your ability to make a break, cross a gap quickly, or attack a hill; it is also particularly valuable for short-distance time triallists and kilometre riders. Use a gear which is tough for getting away fast, but will not produce over-revving at maximum speed. Fast pedalling has its place in producing *souplesse,* but is of little use if you are prettily pedalling your way out of the back of the bunch.

By intermixing these training methods, and taking into account the need for progression, you will build up a good training plan. To get the best from your training, take plenty of good rest, keep to a good diet, and have a regular life-style.

When developing a training plan, it is well to spend some time working out what kind of training has benefitted you in the past. Some riders thrive on long distances, others on a series of short, hard efforts; so it is wise to find out what makes you tick – and not just what you like.

The crowning principle is to make training tougher and tougher, and faster and faster.

Fartlek training imitates the movements of road racing at a more leisurely pace, and can be a useful mode of training once you have achieved a high level of fitness. Note the riders' sensible clothing.

The cyclist's 'high'

The typical cyclist is happy with long, steady distance work and is reluctant to tackle high-intensity work; but when he does get into high levels of training, this has some strange and interesting effects.

High levels of training have been shown to stimulate the production in the body of morphine-like substances called endorphins. These have an opiate effect on the nervous system so that you feel less pain and experience a general feeling of well-being. This is known as the cyclist's 'high'.

The technical background of this is that the Beta endorphin is a 30-amino-acid sequence, and within it are found enkephalins, a 5-amino-acid sequence which mimics the structure of morphine, and thus has a parallel effect in dulling pain and giving a 'high'.

This is why riders who have been competing and training at high levels seem to benefit more from their efforts, and can push themselves to even further limits with a kind of fierce enthusiasm.

How training works

Anyone contemplating some new kind of physical effort and its accompanying training programme should ideally be able to obtain a medical report to confirm that his heart, lungs and body chemistry are able to withstand it. The older you are, the more important this becomes; and it certainly removes any nagging doubts about your health, thus allowing you to attack your training plan with 100-per-cent confidence.

So go to your GP and ask him for a medical – and expect, of course, to have to pay for the service. You will want him to check your blood pressure and the efficiency of your lungs; he should take a blood test and a urine test to check your haemoglobin level, and detect any possible signs of inflammation anywhere in your system; he should also check for any problems with your body chemistry. Your doctor will want to know the reason for your request, so that if any abnormality is revealed he can tell you whether or not you are still able to tackle a training programme – and if not, whether the ban is permanent or temporary.

If training is to be effective, it has to be progressive. You have to aim for a 'progressive overload' so that

each outing pushes you a little further towards peak fitness.

This doesn't mean going out every time to smash yourself into the ground, since such sessions may not (and at any early stage will not) allow you to recover quickly. It is essential that you recover from one training session before the next one begins, otherwise you will be tearing yourself down instead of building yourself up. Later on, when you are approaching your peak state of fitness, there will be plenty of opportunity to strive to reach your physical and mental limits at every outing. But when your programme is just beginning, you are training for general fitness.

It may surprise you to know that you can train for general fitness either on or off the bike. 'Getting in the miles' has for years been the way of achieving general condition, but this method is time-consuming and prone to disruption through winter weather. You can reach a similar general condition by introducing gym work, home exercises and – most important at this stage of preparation – stretching exercises.

Don't underestimate the value of stretching exercises. Most sportsmen – and not only cyclists – tend to have understretched muscles. Only if your muscles are fully stretched, and your joints are fully flexible, can you expect to produce maximum power.

The cycle of training and racing spans a full twelve months of every year, as the facing table illustrates. It shows that there is no such thing as an 'off-season', and that when one racing season ends, preparation for the next one should start.

You can train on the bike throughout the year, depending on the weather and the targets you have set. The actual type of on-the-bike training will vary from initial steady-state long-slow-distance work at the beginning, through to high-intensity training when the season gathers momentum.

This programme is for road, track and time-trial riders. Cyclo-cross men follow a similar twelve-month plan, but their winter-orientated racing means a reversal of the months involved. Their season ends and preparation begins at the end of February, and racing starts in September.

Right at the beginning of your on-the-bike training, assuming that you haven't been out on the bike for a long time (or perhaps not at all), you might simply go out for a gentle ride – a 'potter'. This isn't training in the strict sense of the word, but it does set a level for improvement. You get used to the mechanics of riding a bike, and your muscles get used to working at a regular rate of pressure.

Once this first hurdle is behind you, you can go for a decent steady ride. Steady-state riding, gradually building up in distance, allows you to eliminate the effects of local muscular fatigue, which is the first limiting factor. 'Local muscular fatigue' simply means that your legs hurt!

Those early days of on-the-bike training can be exhilarating or they

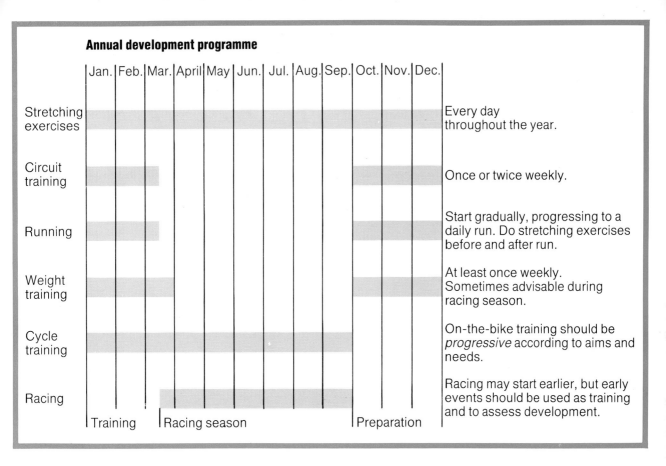

Annual development programme

	Jan.	Feb.	Mar.	April	May	Jun.	Jul.	Aug.	Sep.	Oct.	Nov.	Dec.	
Stretching exercises	████████████████████████████████████												Every day throughout the year.
Circuit training	███									███			Once or twice weekly.
Running	███									███			Start gradually, progressing to a daily run. Do stretching exercises before and after run.
Weight training	███									███			At least once weekly. Sometimes advisable during racing season.
Cycle training	████████████████												On-the-bike training should be *progressive* according to aims and needs.
Racing			███████████████████										Racing may start earlier, but early events should be used as training and to assess development.

Training	Racing season	Preparation

can be disappointing, depending on whether or not you have correctly assessed your state of unfitness. Whatever else, don't finish one ride feeling bad, and then go out the next day and flog yourself even harder, hoping to train through the fatigue. When you first start, it's probably best to train no more than once every other day.

Your resting pulse rate is a good guide to whether you have recovered from the previous day's training session. You should know your resting pulse and monitor it twice daily: once in bed before you rise in the morning, and once after an evening rest. If your pulse is up, then you probably haven't properly recovered – unless there are other reasons for it being elevated, such as a sudden awakening, or a heavy meal late the previous evening. Get used to listening to your body, and heed what it says. If after a training session your morning resting pulse is back to normal, then you can train at that level and higher. If it is still elevated, then you should either rest that day or have an easy session.

If your programme of steady-state work progresses at the right rate, your resting pulse rate will gradually get slower. That is really encouraging, because it means that your heart has been trained to cope more readily with the everyday task of keeping your body going. During steady-state riding you are getting the muscles and their fibres used to regular contractions; you are developing your heart and lungs because of the pressure you are putting on them. You are also improving your body chemistry, so that the toxic effects of effort – like the exhaust fumes emitted by a car – are eliminated far more easily.

This is why a well-trained rider

can happily cruise at 20mph, while a less well-trained rider could well be gasping with the same effort. His system has been trained to cope with the effort much more readily.

Herein lies the difference between aerobic and anaerobic training. The same effort can produce an aerobic or anaerobic effect, depending on the rider's state of fitness. The well-trained rider handles 20mph aerobically: the body ticks over happily and can do so virtually indefinitely. The lesser rider is training anaerobically – going into oxygen debt in an attempt to keep going. It is not just a question of the muscles not being sufficiently trained: the whole system is simply not as well prepared.

It is useful to look at how various forms of training affect the heart. When you are riding steady state, the heart is working within itself. The effort imposed lifts the number of heartbeats per minute – the heart rate – so that enough blood is pumped around the system to cope with the demands of the muscles. The blood carries to the muscles the oxygen needed to keep them working.

Through steady-state riding the chamber of the heart – its internal capacity – is increased. This means that more blood is pumped around the system with each heartbeat, so that fewer beats per minute are needed to cope with a given effort. This is why, over a period, your resting pulse rate goes down.

As you change your training pattern and incorporate some high-intensity training – an effort which takes your pulse rate above 150 – then it is not the chamber which develops, but the cardiac muscle – the actual muscle wall of

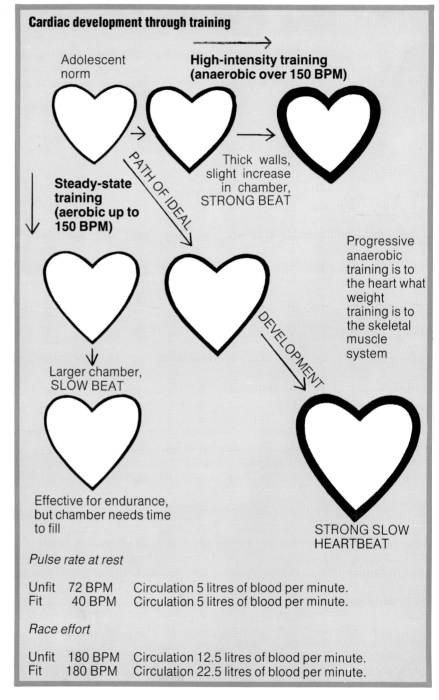

Cardiac development through training

Adolescent norm

High-intensity training (anaerobic over 150 BPM)

PATH OF IDEAL

Steady-state training (aerobic up to 150 BPM)

Thick walls, slight increase in chamber, STRONG BEAT

Progressive anaerobic training is to the heart what weight training is to the skeletal muscle system

Larger chamber, SLOW BEAT

DEVELOPMENT

Effective for endurance, but chamber needs time to fill

STRONG SLOW HEARTBEAT

Pulse rate at rest

Unfit	72 BPM	Circulation 5 litres of blood per minute.
Fit	40 BPM	Circulation 5 litres of blood per minute.

Race effort

Unfit	180 BPM	Circulation 12.5 litres of blood per minute.
Fit	180 BPM	Circulation 22.5 litres of blood per minute.

the heart. This effectively increases the strength of the heart beat.

So steady-state training followed by high-intensity training first increases the heart's capacity and then increases its ability at each stroke to push that increased capacity into the arteries.

A rider who trains only at steady state will simply increase the size of the heart chamber. He will be able to ride for long distances at a steady speed, but will be unable to react to sudden extra demands on the body, such as those imposed in a road race when a breakaway attempt suddenly leaves a gap to be closed. This is one of the reasons why, in the very early stages of training, the slightest increase of pace or adverse gradient has drastic effects. Your body chemistry can't cope; your circulation isn't efficient enough; your muscles can't perform well enough; your lungs can't take up enough oxygen to pass round. In short, the whole body is under-performing, and you just develop heavy legs.

But as the time goes on, these problems lessen. Everybody benefits from high-intensity training because this trains the body to go fast, and racing is about going fast.

But don't be tempted to take short cuts by going straight to high-intensity training without a basis of steady-state work. Your body will simply be unable to cope, and you will very quickly tear yourself down.

So when do you start high-intensity training? The answer is almost cryptic: when you're ready, you'll know. Before this point, you will have felt yourself improving: you will have established all-round basic fitness; you will have been able to make efforts up hills; your pulse rate will have been coming down considerably – and it's then that you must concentrate on race speed.

At this stage you should first cut down your training distance and go for faster rides before moving on to real high-intensity work. You should be training faster but over less distance, so the effort is still aerobic – within your oxygen uptake. Once you have mastered this intermediate stage of training, you can move into a programme based on high-intensity work.

As a general rule, you will need two clear months of pre-season training before you can start high-intensity work, which in turn should start shortly before the actual racing season.

So the broad progression of on-the-bike training is as follows:

1. Basic conditioning training
2. Speed training
3. High-intensity training

This is a definite progression, with each stage merging easily into the next when your body is ready.

Keep a training diary

A training and racing diary is valuable firstly in that it provides positive evidence of how much training you have actually done. You might have set yourself a training plan over a three-week period, but for some reason or other your progress has been impaired by illness, visitors or unexpected commitments. The tendency is to tell yourself that you have virtually followed your programme when in fact you might have fallen considerably short. The diary eliminates the guesswork. You can tell the types of training you have done, how many miles and for how long you have ridden.

The diary helps you follow the progress of your weight and your pulse, which are both excellent indicators of fitness. If you come up against a problem such as overtraining and staleness, or your performances are not as expected, then you can look back in your training diary and plot the causes.

Every day you should record your times of rising and retiring, and record your pulse first thing in the morning and last thing at night. Your weight should be noted twice a week, always at the same time of day and using the same scales. You need to record the type of training and how well you performed it. Put down who your training partners were, and relate your performance to them. This gives you an idea in retrospect of the kind of pressure you sustained.

Describe the race or run, how you felt, how well you recovered. If it's a race, always note the first three finishers, as this will be useful for comparison with your later performances. Note the weather too. Here is a sample training diary entry.

When racing ends, the hard work starts

At the end of a hard racing season, the temptation is always strong to let everything go: stop training, start socialising, and generally do everything that you wouldn't do while you are fully in training.

Psychologically you may need some kind of relaxation, but physically it isn't a good idea to abandon everything with the promise to yourself that you will start training again after a good Christmas blow-out.

And don't be fooled either when you hear top Continentals saying that they don't touch a bike from the end of the last race until New Year's Day. If that is true, then they will certainly not be resting, and their training will be carrying on in some form or other. Some top Continentals tackle cyclo-cross – and certainly it didn't do Roger De Vlaeminck any harm. Bernard Hinault and Freddy Maertens used to run a lot, through woods or over sand dunes. Others seek some sun in the West Indies or the Pacific. Still others go winter-sporting, using the strenuous techniques of cross-country skiing to keep themselves in shape.

While there is no vital need to keep cycling through the off-season, it is frankly a senseless waste not to make an effort to hold on to your basic fitness once racing has finished for the year. And it is certainly easier to recover from staleness than start training from scratch again.

Once you stop doing anything of a physical nature, you will suffer a gradual deterioration – the opposite, in fact, of the training process. Even though initially the deterioration is almost undetectable, it will become more and more evident the longer the lay-off. The deterioration is all-round. You've done all that work to build up your muscles, your body chemistry, your heart and lung functions; and all this starts to go into reverse the moment you discontinue training. Don't you think that's a big waste of effort?

Everything you let slip during the winter has to be earned again in the following year's training. It naturally follows that if you can keep most of your physical condition, then you start your serious training from a higher level, reach your previous peak fitness level more quickly and easily, and then go on to greater things. So treat each year's racing as the basis of training for the following year.

Once racing is finished, don't hang up your bike. While the weather still allows it, keep your training going; but intersperse perhaps two or three weekly outings on the bike with other types of sporting activity, such as gym work, squash or badminton – which incidentally is superb for developing the reactions. Swimming and running are both good – even playing football, providing you treat it as an exercise, and not as a full-blooded commitment to the extent that you get injured.

Pursuing other activities has a double purpose. Firstly, it gives you a different kind of challenge, which is good for the mind. Secondly, it can be a positive force in fitness, since other sporting pursuits may allow you to concentrate on various weak points in your make-up which are not easily improved through going out on the bike.

This is why you shouldn't fret when you can't get in some good on-the-bike work. If it's icy or foggy, you're just asking for trouble going out – when you can get in some solid work in the gymnasium without any risk to your health.

Let's look more closely at some types of winter training.

Weight training

One of the four S's of fitness is strength, and one of the best ways of getting stronger is through a strictly-controlled weight-training programme. Just learning a few lifts and spending some time with the weights until you are pleasantly exhausted is not sufficient. Any work with weights must be under the guidance of a coach who has had detailed instruction on weight-training techniques; he must be able to set up a programme suitable to your personal needs, and which is progressive.

You won't necessarily have to work with very big weights; but, as in all forms of training, there must be progression as you develop your strength. You will naturally use bigger weights as your strength develops.

Exactly how you train with weights – whether you use big weights and few repetitions or smaller weights with more repetitions – will depend on what kind of strength you are seeking: whether you want the power of a sprinter or the stamina of a stage-race rider. Generally speaking, weight lifted over a large number of lifts will tend towards

stamina. Concentrating the same total weight over fewer lifts will develop power. But be extremely careful with heavy weights, because here the risk of stress injury is much increased.

More and more sports centres are now equipped with a multi-gym, an apparatus which allows you to perform a variety of weight-training exercises with less danger of injury through misuse. Even here, the techniques of breathing and grip should be followed under qualified guidance.

Most cyclists use weight training to develop the upper body: the shoulders, the arms and the back. Bike work usually takes care of the legs – although sometimes leg-power exercises might be recommended.

Some coaches advocate weight training well into the racing season, but except with track sprinters this is questionable. Once racing has started, you need to devote maximum time to working on the bike, improving your strengths and skills as a racing cyclist.

All weight-training sessions should start and, if possible, also finish with a programme of stretching exercises.

Use fairly light weights at first, which will allow you to concentrate from the beginning on correct lifting techniques to avoid injury.

Aim for about three sessions, evenly-spaced through the week, and gradually work on progressive repetitions and poundages as you become more proficient and strong. Keep a training diary to assist you.

It's not possible to give a 'correct' poundage for every exercise; this should be decided in conjunction with your weight-training coach.

Typical weights are given as a rough guide only. Always err on the light side, and remember that as you progress you will be doing up to 30 repetitions.

Having decided your poundage, you must think of initial repetitions. Bear in mind your fitness or lack of it. What might seem easy at the time could leave you with aching limbs for the rest of the week. For the first few sessions, keep well within your capacities. If you can't do eight repetitions of each exercise, and three sets of exercises, then the weights are too heavy.

Build this up to three sets of ten repetitions; then gradually increase the poundage on eight repetitions, then on ten, and so on.

This kind of work will give you strength and endurance; but if you are aiming for power, then the procedure is somewhat different. Once you have reached a level of proficiency, you should increase the weights but decrease the repetitions to five or even fewer. However, at this stage you *must* have the close attention of a weights coach.

Weight training can be as beneficial to women as to men, and it is used to great effect by Eastern European and American women riders. There is no danger of producing excessively bulky muscles, because of the essential hormone differences between men and women.

Weight training exercises

1. Repetition power cleans

a. In the squat position, grip the bar with knuckles facing outwards ('get set' position).

b. With a single movement, stand up and bring the bar up to the high chest position, with elbows raised.
c. Keeping the bar close to the chest, lower it to thigh level.
d. Return to squat position, with the bar almost touching the floor.

All movements should be brisk and smooth, paying attention to style.
Guide weight (including bar): 25–30 lb

2. Curls

a. From the 'get set' position, with knuckles inwards this time, stand upright, looking straight ahead.
b. Bring the bar up close to your body to the high chest position, elbows raised.
c. Lower elbows, taking the bar downwards close to your body, to thigh position.

Keep your body erect and still during the exercises. Do not swing the bar up.
Guide weight: 25–30 lb

3. Bench press

a. Lie back on the bench, feet on the floor to stabilise. Take the bar from a stand or a helper, with your arms straight, your hands wide apart, and your knuckles facing your head.
b. Lower the bar almost to touch your chest. Immediately press up to extend arms

Guide weight: 35–40 lb

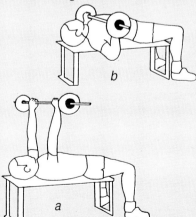

4. Half-squats

a. With your feet a shoulder-width apart, take the bar on to your shoulders from stand or helper, hands wide apart, palms facing forwards. Stand erect, with back straight.

b. Bend knees until thighs are parallel with the ground. You may place a small stool behind you to stop you going down too far, but *don't* sit on it: simply touch it and return to starting position.

Keep your back straight and your heels on the ground throughout.
Guide weight: 65–70 lb

5. Straight-arm pull-overs

This is mainly a breathing exercise.

a. Lie on your back on a bench, with your feet on the floor. Hold the bar with a light weight, hands wide apart, palms facing toes, arms extended vertically upwards.

b. Keeping your arms straight, slowly take the bar back as far as possible, inhaling deeply.

c. Slowly return to starting position while exhaling.
Guide weight: 15 lb

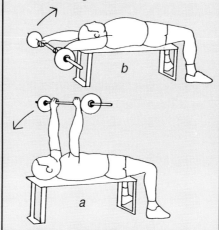

6. Press behind neck

a. Take the bar on to your shoulders from stand or helper, hands wide apart, palms facing forward. Press up to extend arms fully.

b. Lower to starting position. Take care not to hit the back of your neck during either movement.
Guide weight: 25–30 lb

7. Dorsal hyperextensions

a. Lie face down on a bench, hips level with the end, feet secured by a strap or a helper, hands clasped behind your neck. Start by letting the body drop down towards the floor.

b. Raise head and upper body as high as possible.
No weight necessary

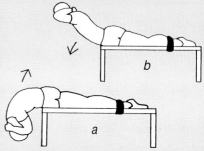

8. Bent-forward rowing

a. Start in the get set position, hands wide apart, knuckles forward. Stand up, bringing bar up to your thighs. Bend forward from the waist, letting the bar hang at arms' length, knees slightly bent.

b. Pull the bar up to touch the chest lightly, then lower.

Keep your head up and trunk motionless throughout the exercise.
Guide weight: 25–30 lb

9. Bent-knee sit-ups

a. Lie on a slightly inclined bench, feet uppermost and secured by a strap, knees bent, hands behind neck.

b. Sit up and touch knees with elbows.

Variation: when sitting up, twist body to touch right knee with left elbow, and vice versa.

Guide weight: none necessary unless you become very proficient

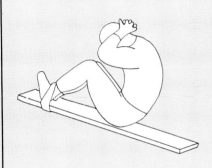

10. Upright rowing

a. Start in the get set position, knuckles forward, hands approximately three inches apart. Stand to bring the bar to your thighs.

b. Turning elbows outwards, lift the bar to beneath the chin, elbows high.

c. Lower the bar to your thighs. Take care not to hit your chin with the bar.

Guide weight: 25–30 lb

Multi-gym

The use of resistance exercise machines such as Multi-gym and Nautilus is becoming more and more widespread as a fitness technique. They offer similar training to weight training, and need to be approached with a similar amount of respect. So no playing about, no competition; just concentrate on following a programme that is right for you. Start with a general stretching programme to warm yourself up.

Weights on the exercise machine are usually printed on the side of the weights themselves. You pick your poundage by inserting the selector pin at the appropriate mark. Always ensure that the selector pin is firmly in place before you start to exercise. Never place your fingers between the weights, or near the pulleys or wires. And never let the weights drop; always let them down under control. If in doubt, always approach the instructor or gym official and get specific advice.

As with weight training, start with a light weight to get used to the exercise, then go through the prescribed circuit. Then gradually increase the poundage until you find the sort of weight which extends you.

The 'circuits' referred to in the context of resistance machines have nothing to do with circuit training, but are the term equivalent to 'sets' in weight training. Here are some exercises of particular use for the cyclist.

Exercises for resistance exercise machines.
Basic circuit

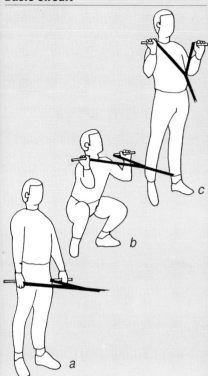

1. Clean from hang

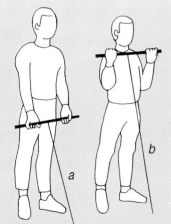

2. Arm curls

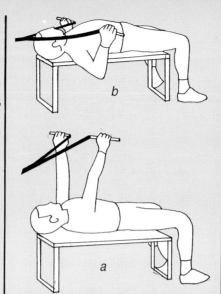

3. Bench press

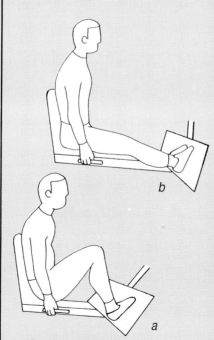

4. Seated leg press
(upper/lower position
single/both legs)

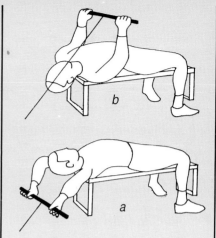

5. Bent-arm pull-over

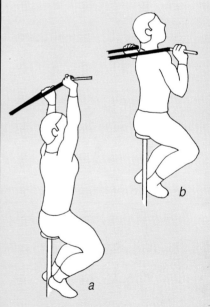

6. Press behind neck

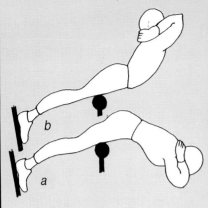

7. Back hyperextension

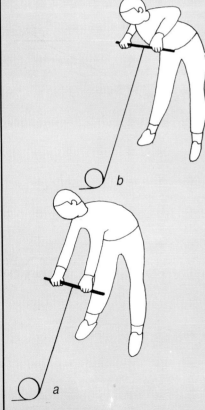

8. Bent-over rowing

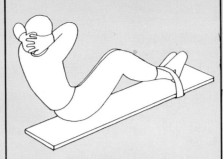

9. Bent-knee sit-ups
(straight or twisting)

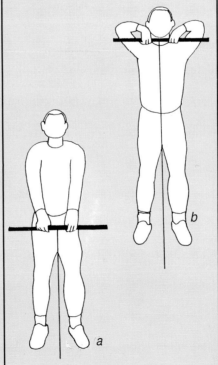

10. Upright rowing

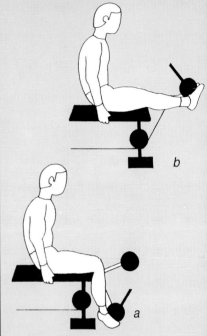

1. Leg extension
(single/both legs)

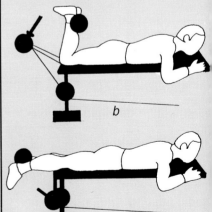

2. Leg curl (single/both legs)

92

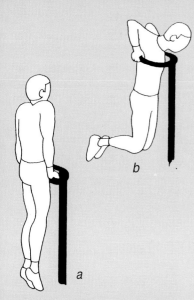

3. Dips (front or reverse grip)

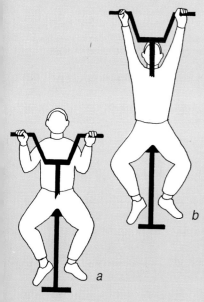

4. Shoulder press

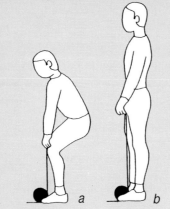

5. Dead lift

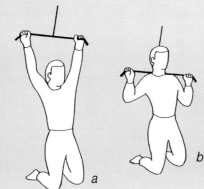

6. Pulldown behind neck
(standing or kneeling)

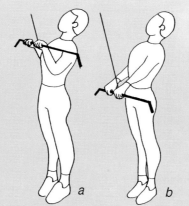

7. Tricep extension

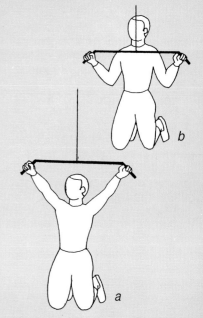

8. Latissimus pulldown
(standing or kneeling)

9. Chins
(front or reverse grip)

93

Circuit training

This is a regime of training for all-round fitness which is highly recommended during the winter. It is a set pattern of exercises arranged in a circuit. This pattern of exercises is tackled in a progressive manner, which brings about an improvement in your general state of fitness.

The ideal circuit in a gymnasium uses apparatus set out to exercise different muscle groups in turn. The first exercise might put pressure on the arms, the next on the legs, the next on the back, and so on.

You perform each exercise in turn with a brief, timed rest in between. Once you have completed the exercise circuit, you try a second or a third circuit. You can make circuit training progressive, either by aiming to finish your circuits more quickly, or by doing more repetitions of each exercise, or eventually by doing a fourth circuit – or a third if you have only managed two circuits at first.

Circuit training is tough. If you don't find it tough, then you aren't trying hard enough. With a warm-up in the gym (not forgetting your stretching exercises) – followed by the circuits, and then a gentle warm-down, you will have done about an hour's hard work – and that's plenty.

Another advantage of circuit training is that it can develop your competitive nature. You generally move around the gym in company with others doing the same exercise, and you will naturally work to do more repetitions than your fellow-travellers – that is, if you're the type of rider who is aggressive on a bike.

Don't worry if you can't find a circuit-training venue which caters specially for cyclists. It just isn't necessary, because the aim is all-round fitness, and that aim is the same for any sportsman. In fact you can probably benefit from mixing with people who play other sports.

Exercises at home

This is a vital part of your training regime, not just in the winter but in the summer too. Home exercises should once again be progressive, increasing the repetitions, or sets of repetitions, gradually. And the ideal programme must include a good proportion of stretching exercises.

Daily stretching and exercising should become a part of your way of life. Why not do them first thing in the morning, on an empty stomach? They will help you to wake up and get into the day's business quicker and better.

Stretching promotes a fully flexible body with the greatest possible range of movement, and therefore a body which can develop the greatest power from its strength. Flexibility is important in all sports, and can be a great advantage in cycle racing. If you are fully flexible you run much less risk of muscle strains and muscle soreness; your circulation is better and your muscles will perform more efficiently.

Apart from your daily stretching routine, you should also perform stretching exercises before and after any gym work or running. Exercise stretches muscles, but a sudden launching into exercise can provoke muscle spasms (cramp) or muscle injury – hence the need for stretching exercises before effort,

to introduce the muscles gently to the idea of effort.

Hard work by muscles tends to make them shorten as fatigue sets in, and again there is a danger of cramp attacks soon after the effort is finished. This is why you must stretch afterwards, gently extending the shortened muscles in a controlled way. Incidentally, this is also one reason for warming down on the bike at the end of a tough race or training session.

Static stretching is a safe and simple process if you follow these simple rules:

1. Do it slowly. Follow the exercise procedure to the point of stretch (not pain) and hold for 30–60 seconds.
2. Don't hurry though the exercises. Concentrate on relaxing.
3. If one particular muscle group is tight, then perform the appropriate stretches several times during the day, until the tightness eases.
4. If you are injured, keep stretching during recovery. However, don't persist with any stretching exercise which causes pain in the area of injury. But the moment the pain disappears, stretch again.
5. Stretch and flexibility will develop gradually. The more regular your stretching programme, the better the results.
6. Stretching isn't a competitive activity. Some individuals start with more flexibility than others. So work to your limits and ability, and not to those of others.

Static stretching exercises

Here is a routine to follow at least daily:

1. Shoulder stretch

Stand with your feet slightly apart, arms extended in front with fingers interlaced. Roll the palms away from you and lift your arms up and over your head as far as possible, keeping the chin tucked in. Feel the stretch in your shoulders and sides. (See *a* and *b* below.)

Then stretch the opposite way. Stand with your feet slightly apart, arms behind, fingers interlaced. Now roll your palms towards you and lift your arms as far as possible. When you reach the limit of your stretch, bend forward at the waist and stretch your arms still further upwards (see *c* below).

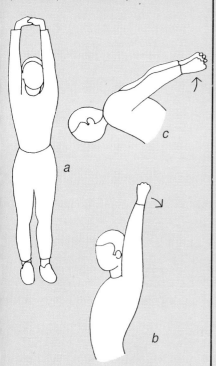

2. Lateral stretch

Stand with your feet slighly apart and arms at sides. Extend one arm above your head while sliding the other palm as far as possible down the outside of the leg. Keep your head up and avoid bending forward. Feel the stretch at your side. Repeat on the other side.

3. Calf stretch

Stand about a metre from a wall. Rest the forearms vertically against the wall. Keep your body in a straight line, with your bottom tucked in and heels on the floor. Feel the stretch on your calf muscles. Hold for 30 seconds.

4. Quadriceps stretch

Stand beside a chair or wall (for balance). Bend the outside knee backwards and the foot up towards the buttock. Grasp your ankle. Pull gently on your ankle towards the buttock and at the same time arch your back. Feel the stretch down the front of your thigh. Turn round and repeat the exercise on the other leg.

5. Hamstring stretch

Place your feet just more than shoulder-width apart. Keeping your legs straight, bend forward to clasp the leg above the ankle with both hands. Slide your hands downwards until you feel the stretch on your hamstrings. Bend your elbows to pull yourself smoothly downwards and accentuate the stretch. Repeat on other side.

6. Adductor stretch
Stretch one leg out sideways. Bend the other knee. Lean towards the bent knee to feel the stretch on the inside of the thigh. Repeat the exercise on the other side.

7. Lumbar and hip stretch
Lie on your back. Bring both knees up to your chest. Hold both knees in with your hands and bend your head down to touch your knees. Feel the stretch in your hips and lower back.

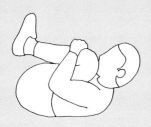

Some of these exercises are used in yoga routines aimed at promoting physical flexibility, and you will find much in common between your aims and the aims of those who follow yoga disciplines. It is important to breathe evenly during your routine, and to relax while performing the movements. This will allow you to stretch most effectively.

After your stretching exercises in the morning, move on to the following exercises for a further 20 minutes.

Home circuit training

1. Star jumps
Start with hands on hips and sink into squat position. Leap into the air, flinging your arms and legs out into star shape. Sink back into squat position.

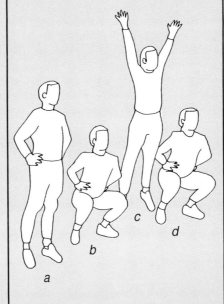

2. Press-ups
Lie face down on floor. Place your hands at chest level. Straighten your arms, lifting your body at the same time. Keep your body straight at all times. If you are very weak, keep your knees on the ground.

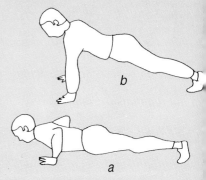

3. Squat thrusts
Start in press-up position with your arms straight. Jump forward with your feet until your knees are between your arms; then jump back, thrusting your legs straight back in the process.

4. Leg raises

Lie on back on floor with your arms by your sides. Lift your legs slowly until they form an angle of 45 degrees with floor. Lower them slowly.

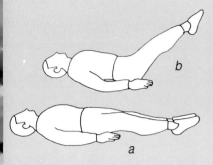

6. Bent-knee sit-ups

Hook your feet under a firm object such as a radiator or a sofa. Lie on your back with your hands clasped behind your neck. Curl up to a sitting position. Then slowly return to the start position.

8. Back lifts

Lie in the prone position with your arms at your sides. Raise your chest and your feet off ground simultaneously, forming a shallow arch with your body.

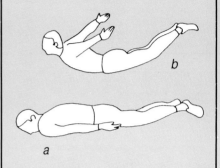

5. Step-ups

Find a stool or box some 15 inches (40 cm) high. Step up on to the box; stand still momentarily on top of the box; then step down. Repeat, changing the leading leg frequently. Do not 'skip' up on to the box, but use a definite one-two-three-four step-up/step-down rhythm.

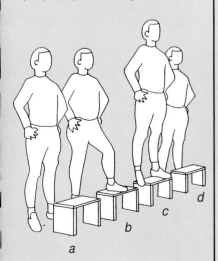

7. Skipping

This can be performed either with or without a rope. Put your hands on your hips if without a rope. Then skip, bringing your knees up high. Don't do boxer skipping, which barely lifts your feet off the ground.

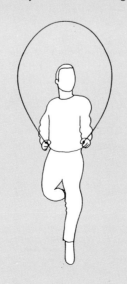

9. Trunk curls

Lie on your back on the floor with your arms straight and your hands on your thighs. Sit up slowly, sliding your hands down your thighs to your knees. Return slowly to starting position.

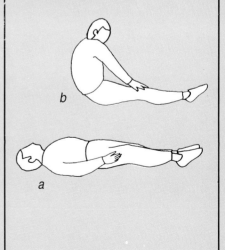

10. Heel raises

Use a small block of wood. Position your toes and the balls of both feet on the block. Slowly let your heels down to touch the floor; then rise up on tip-toe. Return to starting position.

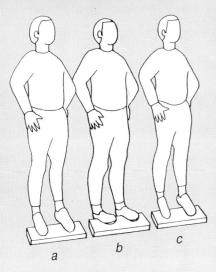

a   b   c

Running

This is a superb form of exercise for the off-season, because it helps to develop the heart and lungs. Running is very efficient as a training medium because you can put your cardio-vascular (heart-lung) system under pressure in a comparatively short time. In a half-hour run you can do the kind of work it would take perhaps two hours' hard riding to achieve. You can imagine how that will help your training programme when time is short or the weather foul! In fact, you can run in conditions which would be really terrible for cycling, and revel in the conditions because your whole body is working and producing warmth. Only desist when it is foggy. If it's icy, then try to run on well-lit grass or soft surfaces. You can come a purler on icy pavements as easily as when riding a bike on icy roads.

However, there are some precautions you must always observe. Stretching is vital before and after a run. If you aren't used to running, then take it gently at first: start with perhaps 15 minutes and work up gradually. A guide would be to increase your mileage by no more than ten per cent each week. Outings of about 40 minutes are very useful. Buy good running shoes with well-cushioned soles, because running on hard pavements can be terribly jarring. A specialist running shop will advise on the choice of shoes. Stay away from heavily-cambered road surfaces, and where there is no pavement always run facing the oncoming traffic. Wear one layer less than you would if you were cycling, and make sure the top layer is light-coloured or has reflective

Professional Sean Yates uses running as a regular part of his winter preparation.

patches. Best of all for running is a circuit of well-beaten paths without ruts or potholes. Beach running is good, too, providing the beach isn't heavily cambered.

Some people will tell you that running isn't good for a cyclist because 'the muscles are exercised differently'. That simply isn't true, because the more you exercise your body in different ways, the more you increase its adaptability – and that can only be good.

Other sports

Swimming is an excellent winter pursuit. It can be done in warm surroundings, it exercises the whole body against resistance (the water), and it is good for developing your breathing.

Racket games – badminton, squash, indoor tennis – develop the heart and all kinds of muscles, as well as the reflexes and co-ordination.

Team games, such as volleyball, basketball and five-a-side football, can all play their part; but try to avoid body contact and consequent injury.

If it takes your fancy, you can even incorporate the ultra-modern craze of aerobic dance routines into your programme, providing the instructor is of proven ability.

Just one word of warning about tackling anything 'different'. You are used to riding a bike, but other forms of exercise should be taken cautiously at first, until you have mastered the techniques involved. Then work progressively, as with your cycling. Don't be tempted into hammering yourself into the ground on your first run, your first weight-training session, and so on. In the end all you will do is stop yourself training for a while.

Roller training

Home trainers (rollers) have very little place in a training programme. They need a considerable investment in time for little return; but they can be used to loosen up your legs after a hard session or a race, to help remove some of the stiffness. Track riders can keep loose by using rollers in between events, when other warm-up facilities are difficult to arrange.

Rollers offer little resistance exercise; they can quickly become boring, and often cause you to sweat profusely, giving a false impression that you are working hard.

Rollers are useful in retaining souplesse *and keeping the muscles warmed up between track events.*

The daily routine

You want to be a champion, and that involves dedication and commitment. This starts with following a daily routine which should become second nature. It should be natural for you to seek some form of exercise every day, unless you have trained for some reason that you haven't recovered from the previous session.

So don't be put off if your training plans are for some reason disturbed. If, on the day you had planned a good outing on the bike, you wake up and find the country six feet deep in snow, then immediately change plans and do something else. If all else fails, then go through your stretching and home exercise routine on three separate occasions during the day – a good half-hour each time. You'll feel the benefit.

And if, despite everything, you have a blank day in your training diary, then don't let it prey on your mind. You won't have lost much. The effect of training lasts some 48 hours before it starts to 'wear off', which means that if you train only once every other day you can still progress, albeit more slowly. If you can train every day, you simply progress a lot faster.

An alternative way of keeping warmed up between track events is to ride a road bike around the track centre, warmly wrapped up if necessary. This is better than rollers because it keep some pressure on the pedalling. Riding around with a team-mate and chatting will also help relieve tension. Here are American women sprinters Sheila Young (left) and Connie Paraskevin.

The build-up to racing

After the first half of winter, which is really only a time for conserving your condition while the weather does its worst, the new year heralds the start of the real pre-season training period. This doesn't mean, however, that you can let everything go until all the Christmas decorations are taken down. On the contrary, you should have been working hard to make sure that you can benefit from your on-the-bike training once it starts to be a major part of your programme.

The start of a new year is a good point psychologically to start concentrating on the bike again, but it is also a logical point for any rider contemplating racing in March. For before you can start the high-intensity training which is the immediate prelude to racing, you need to put in two solid months of riding – steady state at first, and then speed work.

The training bike

When the weather is dismal, it's easy to understand why riders use an old bike for training. It's harder to understand why some seem to glory in having their 'hack' bikes in a terrible state of disrepair. Your training bike should be just as safe and as mechanically sound as the one you race on. You must have good brakes, because you are more likely to be training in bad weather than you are to be racing in it. Your saddle must be good and

comfortable, and it is highly advisable to use mudguards. Resist the temptation to go out without them, even though you might feel it looks better. You will be spending several hours at a time in the saddle on this machine, so you will need all the comfort you can get. Why condemn yourself to a regular soaking from wet roads when you can keep much drier just by fitting guards?

Your riding position should be based on your racing position, but with subtle alterations. Because you will probably be wearing shorts, long johns and track-bottoms or 'plusses', you will be wearing two extra layers of clothing between you and your saddle, so the saddle height must be lowered accordingly. Amazingly, the extra layers of clothing affect your handlebar height too. All those jerseys put more strain on the back of your neck, since you are unconsciously pushing upwards against them. It's a kind of resistance exercise which you can do without, so raise your bars a little to compensate.

Your winter bike will obviously weigh more, with its heavier tyres and wheels, but this isn't important. Indeed, when you switch to your racing bike for later training outings, the sudden extra responsiveness of the lighter machine will provide a morale-booster.

It used to be traditional that winter training would be done on a single fixed gear (or single freewheel). Unless you are a track rider or a time triallist aiming at racing on a fixed wheel, then this kind of step has little relevance – unless, of course, you are trying to break a habit of big-gear riding by simply removing the temptation! Using your derailleur properly is a skill, and you have to rediscover the feel of gear-changing every season.

Gearing

There is no hard and fast rule about the size of gears to use during training – although the 'favourite' of the professional riders is around 44 x 18 (66 inches). The important point is to choose a gear which you can 'feel'. The use of big or little gears will vary from person to person, depending on their pedalling technique. You should simply use a gear which you can turn smoothly, but which provides some slight resistance. Typically, you should be pedalling at around 70–80 revs per minute. When you are racing you will often rev faster than this, but there are no grounds for going out and 'twiddling' in training, just for the hell of it. Even with superbly supple riders, anything above about 120rpm is inefficient.

When you start doing speed work and high-intensity training, then you push your gears up accordingly, but beware of aiming for high gears and equating them with high speed. It isn't necessarily so. Always pedal at the rate which is most efficient for you, and use the gear which fits that rhythm.

One departure from this rule is when you use over-high gears for a specific purpose. You might be using them to develop power: for example, when you try to jump away up a hill from a very slow pace – which will benefit sprinters, kilometre men, or roadmen seeking a finishing sprint. Another time to use bigger gears is when you are consciously trying to work on your ability to pull up on one pedal as you

push down on the other, a technique which brought Frenchman Jacques Anquetil a fantastic record in time trials. The ability to pedal at maximum output for virtually a whole revolution is something worth striving for. Most people use only half their power by only pushing down on the pedals, and not pulling up. There is also a problem if you get out of the saddle awkwardly: this actually checks your pedalling because your body weight is suddenly coming down against a rising pedal.

Clothing for training

There is little point, when you are out to train your body, in using energy just to keep warm – which is what happens when you go out training with insufficient clothing. The principle is always to err on the side of over-dressing. So dress to be warm from the beginning of your training session, and wear clothes that can take care of the sweat you will produce.

Always wear some kind of woolly hat, preferably with a peak, and enough excess material that can be folded down over the ears and the back of the neck if required. You lose a massive amount of body heat through an uncovered head. The hat also stops sweat running into your eyes, and the peak can keep off the worst of the rain or keep the sun out of your eyes.

Your biggest enemy in keeping warm is the wind, which always makes a day effectively colder than it feels when you are standing still. It would seem an obvious idea to wear one of those light nylon jackets or anoraks, but this simply

leads to overheating because the body cannot breathe. Use them only as a last resort in ice-cold weather, or as a conserver of heat if you have been forced to stop for a time.

No, stop the wind by building up a defence in layers. Start with a short-sleeved vest next to the skin; this should be of an absorbent natural fibre like wool or cotton (not nylon), or possibly of the current fabrics which wick the perspiration away from the skin and hence stop you feeling clammy. Then start building up layer upon layer of old racing jerseys – ideal because of their length – until you have the right level of warmth. It isn't unusual in the depths of winter to be wearing five or six layers. Wherever possible, choose jerseys with a good wool content, which absorb sweat better. On days of biting wind, slip a folded newspaper in between two of the jerseys, to give added protection to the chest. You could alternatively use track tops with windproof nylon fronts. If you are wearing several layers, however, make sure that the effect is not one of a corset which constricts your breathing. Jerseys for training can be a size bigger than those used close to the skin for racing.

On the lower half, start with a pair of racing shorts, and make sure that the chamois insert is good. Then add long underpants or ski tights if it's really cold, and always woolly tights on top. If you prefer to ride with 'plusses' (knee-length trousers) then combine them with long woollen socks. Given that you're wearing shorts next to the skin (never underpants, which can ruck up and cause chafing and soreness) it's important that they should be close-fitting and of a dense material, so as to stop the wind getting at your kidneys and groin. Make sure that the waistband isn't tight, because you don't want the circulation to your lower limbs restricted.

For a similar reason, use braces to hold up your tights or plusses, which also ensures that there is no gap between them and the jersey at the back when you are bent forward.

Incidentally, don't shy away from putting embrocation on your back and over your knees in very cold weather, even though they are protected by several layers. A dab of Vick, camphorated oil or Olbas oil (a herbal oil preparation) on your chest will help to keep your nose unclogged.

If your jerseys aren't high cut at the neck, then press a woolly scarf into service. Wear gloves or mittens (two pairs if it's very cold) which are long enough not to leave a gap at the wrists (another potential point of heavy heat loss).

You have plenty of choice in footwear. You can go for specially high-cut cycling shoes (bootees) if you don't find them restrictive, and these should have shoe-plates too. You can use unperforated shoes, or racing shoes with the extra protection of either a pair of shoe-covers (widely available) or simply a pair of woollen socks pulled over the top. Remember that if you are wearing thick socks, then your normal shoes may be too tight and restrict the circulation.

A racing cape should always be taken on training runs as a last resort in case the weather turns very wet. It can be carried rolled up underneath the saddle or in a bottle cage, and should only be used if it seems you will be out in the rain long enough for the wet to find its way through all your protective layers.

Monitoring your progress

Once you get used to riding regularly again, you will start to feel the progress of your training, through the snap of your pedal-thrust, the sharpness of your recovery, the slowness of your pulse rate and the strength of its beat.

On the other hand, watch out for warning signs. Perhaps after two hard training days you won't have recovered properly – and, strange to say, one of the signs of this is that you don't sleep. Your body is upset, and sometimes you unaccountably break into a body sweat and ache all over. Your body has started to generate more and more heat in a bid to sweat out the toxins which overtraining has left. In short, you have developed a slight fever.

Your weight is also a guide. For a while you should be losing weight as you lose body fat, but there comes a point when you can actually start to gain weight as you put on more muscle. So don't be demoralised if you stop losing weight for no apparent reason. In fact the weight you are gaining is highly productive. However, beware of any sudden gain or loss in body weight, as this can be a warning sign.

Take stock again

The more you want, the harder you have to work for it. This is a basic truth of life, and certainly of cycling. So it helps to take stock as you contemplate the run-up to another season. Are you happy just to be club champion? If not, then you'll need to train harder; if you want a division championship, then harder still; and if your goal is a world crown, then the intensity of training, the dedication, the concentration and the time involved all must increase accordingly.

So don't kid yourself, as so many do. So many riders just 'get the miles in' and reject speed training, interval training – all the areas of progression – because these require a greater commitment in effort. As a result, they just train themselves to a plateau of mediocrity. It is so easy to go out with training partners who aren't up to your level, so that you can ride them off your wheel when you please. It is easy, but it isn't the answer. If this is the way you train, then you are in fact relying haphazardly on the actual racing to really extend you and bring you some form. You are 'racing yourself fit', which means that the racing itself – not a progressive training plan – decides whether and when you will start to improve.

If you are to improve steadily, then you must systematically and regular extend yourself. Do it, and revel in the pain you cause yourself – because in the pain lies the improvement. At the same time, it helps you to assess whether you are following the right path within cycling – whether the particular speciality you have chosen is really right for you.

If you are a thin, weedy rider, unless you train for strength the top events just aren't for you. If you are heavy, you can rule out hill-climbs or stage races which include a lot of hilly terrain, because your power-weight ratio is wrong for them.

Plan your season

Now that you have got Christmas behind you, you will obviously be tempted to throw everything into on-the-bike training. But that isn't a good idea. Even if you have been able to get in three or four good rides most weeks leading up to Christmas, you will not be ready for the big training mileages day after day. So start gently, even riding only an hour at first if necessary, and work up to the long rides of five or six hours (which is what the professionals do) when you are fully able to take them in your stride.

At the beginning of January you are still very much in the preparation stage. The weather can still turn nasty and invariably does, so content yourself with increasing the on-the-bike content without completely abandoning all other forms of training.

By now you will probably have access to the racing dates for the coming year, and this should give you your major goals – the times when you should be peaking. You will thus be able to plan your training in more detail, whether you are after a club championship or an Olympic gold.

However, don't fall into the trap of being inflexible in your training routine. As the year goes on there can be setbacks – or what appear to be setbacks. You might be selected to go on an international race, which means you are away from your normal training routine and environment. In such circumstances it's not unknown for riders to 'talk themselves unfit' – persuade themselves that they are losing fitness because they are not following their set programme of so many laps of a given road circuit. This is all despite the fact that top-class racing will have effectively given them high-quality training! Be aware all the time of what a particular exercise – be it racing or training – is doing for you, even though it may take place in strange surroundings.

The opposite can also take place. Riders on a long international trip such as the world championships, Olympic or Commonwealth Games, may feel that the atmosphere of the occasion will miraculously keep them fit without their having to throw a leg over the saddle.

So once you have mapped out your training plan, be prepared to modify it to take care of unexpected racing trips, illness, even holidays.

Bearing in mind the constant need for flexibility, here is a month-by-month training plan for a club rider aiming at success at division level, assuming that he has already followed a full pre-Christmas routine as described earlier.

January

This is not always a month which is kind to cyclists, so be prepared to modify the pattern of training when the roads are very icy or the air is laden with fog. On such days, stay off the bike: don't go out running, but content yourself with gym work or home exercises.

Mondays: Gym work or weight training
Tuesdays: 2–3 hours on the bike (steady miles)
Wednesdays: Gym/weights
Thursdays: As Tuesdays
Fridays: A lighter session in the gym
Saturdays: 3–4 hours on the bike
Sundays: 4–6 hours on the bike

These on-the-bike sessions should preferably be done in company. It relieves the monotony of pedalling for hours at a stretch. It keeps you going when you might feel like taking it easy. And if you have punctures or other mechanical problems, help is always at hand.

February

Follow a similar programme to January, but remember that sessions should be progressive. You may still be on the bike for the same time, but by now you should be travelling further in that time, because you will be moving at a higher speed.

March

Now the racing period starts, even though you may not choose to enter a competition just yet. The weather will have improved, which makes possible more training on the bike and consequently less training in the gym. But if the weather is really foul, you can still make for the gym instead of the bike shed.

This phase of training, even if it doesn't include racing itself, will at least feature types of on-the-bike work which develop strength (strength-endurance training), or speed work. During this period you should start to taper off the long, steady miles at weekends in favour of more specific training for speed or strength.

Mondays: A recovery day, so a lighter training ride on low gears

Tuesdays: 2–3 hours of general endurance training

Wednesdays: Weights or gym work as previously

Thursdays: 3 hours of long, steady distance, but try to lift the speed a bit, especially towards the end

Fridays: A rest day, but check the bike ready for the weekend

Saturdays: Early-season races – used really as a training exercise, developing techniques and generally pushing back your anaerobic threshold – the point where you gasp for air as you go into oxygen debt

Sundays: Either race as on Saturday, or go for a 5–6 hour ride, putting on the pressure from time to time

April

Mondays: Again a recovery day, so light riding on low gears, spinning the legs to work out some of the lactic acid which will have built up in your legs because of the weekend efforts

Tuesdays: 3 hours on the bike, going out with a group, doing some bit-and-bit riding. If you have to train on your own, really put the pressure on from time to time

Wednesdays: Look for special areas of development. This is usually a good time of year to look for strength-endurance, so train accordingly

Thursdays: 3 hours, as on Tuesdays

Fridays: Check the bike and prepare everything for the coming weekend

Saturdays/Sundays: Racing according to fitness and conditions; otherwise steady riding

May

We are now entering the 'target area', when you start to ride the major events. These major events put you under pressure which, combined with heavy training, could bring recovery problems; so at this period specially, it is important to check your pulse twice daily to see whether you have recovered from the previous work. If at any time your pulse is unaccountably elevated, then your next day's training should be lighter than normal.

By now, too, the weather should be much better, and you get the added boost of sun on your face after months of cold, wet and wind. However, resist the temptation to go out in shorts, because your muscles won't thank you! Only train in shorts when it is really hot.

Mondays: Recovery or, if you haven't raced at the weekend, specialised on-the-bike training according to need – preferably strength-endurance

Tuesdays: Approximately 1½ hours of paced effort, as fast as you can. This is a preparation for even greater speed later in the programme

Wednesdays: General anaerobic endurance work, about 3 hours, putting on the pressure from time to time to make sure you go into anaerobic condition. This gets your muscles used to working with a build-up of lactic acid

Thursdays: By this time of the season track leagues have started, so this would be profitable training. Otherwise, speed training

Fridays: Checking the bike and preparing for the weekend

Saturdays/Sundays: Racing

June

Follow the May programme until mid-June, which is really the start of the year's most important period, with championships coming up at all levels. Then as follows:

Mondays: Recovery or training for speed

Tuesdays: General anaerobic endurance work

Wednesdays: 4 hours' steady riding

Thursdays: Track racing or interval training

Fridays: Prepare for the weekend

Saturdays/Sundays: Racing

July – August

This sort of programme should be gradually stepped up so that it places more and more emphasis on anaerobic work – interval training according to your particular needs.

Watch out during this time for signs of staleness, which might show itself through loss of sleep, loss of appetite, general irritability and loss of form. If these signs are present but only slightly, then just ease up on training slightly. But if the symptoms are very pronounced, then give up bike training for a while: go to the theatre or watch a movie – do something to take your mind off the bike for a while and refresh yourself mentally. Make sure that you stay on a good

Winter training requires proper warm, protective clothing from top to toe, and a reliable machine.

Professional roadmen like Greg Lemond spend many hours in the saddle during pre-season training. It is the basis of their preparation, and can often involve six-hour rides in all conditions. But at least they have a team manager to keep them at it. Cyrille Guimard from Renault hands out a racing cape from the team vehicle.

Below left: Marianne Martin of the USA, who won the first women's Tour de France and showed the strength of women's racing in her country. The 'best' riders weren't even sent to the French event, since they were preparing for the Olympics.

Below right: Londoner Paul Bennett is a great example of dedication among veteran riders. A former British competition record-holder at 25 miles, he came back as a veteran to beat his previous record time.

Facing: Professional riders will 'peak' for the Tour de France, but this race in turn will sharpen their fitness for the world championship which follows some six weeks later

Overleaf: In hot events like the Tour de France, fluid loss through sweating is a big problem. Here a spectator offers mineral water to ace climber Lucien Van Impe.

diet, get some early nights and take an increased supplement of vitamin B complex (about 100mg daily) plus a daily gram of vitamin C. These vitamins will aid recovery from staleness. Since both these vitamins are water-soluble, they can pose no problems of overdosing.

This kind of training level will continue to the end of August, until you have completed your major races. By this time you should start to taper off your training.

As the season finishes, then you come once again to the winter phase of recuperation and preparation for the following season, during which you can ride your bike purely for leisure, and start taking an interest in other sports. This is not just to give yourself a rest from cycling. Cyclists do have a tendency to wrap themselves up completely in the subculture of the sport, and lose sight of other factors. The contact with other sports can develop a greater level of ambition than would be accepted within cycling circles.

During this tapering-off period, while the memories are still fresh, try to analyse the season which has ended: identify the mistakes and problems, and plan how to overcome them next season.

Finally, it is important to remember that this suggested training programme is just a broad outline and is for the road rider aiming for success at division level. It can be altered or adapted for different needs. This programme presupposes about 6–8 training sessions weekly; but a beginner, for example, might go out only 3–5 times weekly.

We shall now go on to consider how to adapt the programme for other classes of rider.

Schoolboys

If you are a young teenager, you should plan your programme with great care. First you need to assess your level of physical development, and also whether you have some kind of fitness from doing other sports. Once again, remember that training must be progressive. It can start as early as 12, but from this age to about 15, you have to consider the effects of puberty on your body as you try to train it.

It is usually just before 12 that you get a 'growth spurt' and puberty starts, bringing with it a host of hormonal, biochemical and physiological changes. As a result of these changes your body can't cope with high-intensity work in the way that an adult can. During puberty, and even in the years immediately following, the body does not function properly with high levels of lactic acid. It cannot tolerate the effects of interval training, and the increased levels of lactic acid in the muscles that it brings. There is really no reason to start serious high-intensity work before the age of 17. By all means do speed work, but stay away from interval training.

The emphasis should be on steady distance work with some progressive speed-endurance work. You can do some sprinting of short duration, because here the period of anaerobic effort would not last long.

Schoolboys should undertake a gentle stretching routine every day, because hard work during training can cause muscles to contract afterwards. Given that at this age your bones are often growing in advance of your muscles, there is often a chance of restriction or even pain around the joints – 'growing pains' – so it is important not to accentuate this by shortening muscles still further. Keep well stretched and flexible, by exercising regularly and gently, and you will reduce the likelihood of such problems.

As a general guideline – and it can only be general because in early teenage the biological age is not always consistent with chronological age – restrict training during pre-puberty to mostly aerobic work. This means steady state, 'getting in the miles'. Take this opportunity to learn the 'game' of bike riding – braking, cornering, general techniques and skills.

During puberty itself, continue the aerobic work, but bring in some sprints and a little anaerobic work – though not to the extent that the muscles are being asked to work with high levels of lactic acid. They simply would not work efficiently, and this would bring unwarranted disappointment. Carry on perfecting the skills.

Once puberty is past, you can increase your sprints and speed work, and do more anaerobics; but only now should you start to experiment with various types of racing with a view to eventual specialisation.

Schoolboy racing. At this age physiques will vary immensely depending on how much the individual has matured.

Veterans

Very few over-40s come to cycling with no experience at all. Usually they have raced in the past and given up cycling for various reasons, or they have given up racing but have continued with cycling on a non-competitive level. So most of them have some knowledge of themselves.

This isn't always a good thing. The science of training has advanced so much in recent years that all the old standards have been swept away; yet many vets return to cycling with pre-conceived notions based on what used to happen.

Naturally it's tough for vets to improve on past performances. It's much harder for a vet to improve his cardio-respiratory (heart-lung) fitness than it would be for a younger person. His chest cage is already fully developed and is no longer as flexible, and the heart muscle will have reduced its efficiency in some respects because of the break in training. As a result, any development will have to be slow.

Now that over-40 racing is well established, there are many riders who never stop racing and thus don't make a comeback as a vet. They simply start to blend in veteran events with their existing racing programme, in which they may still be winning against riders half their age. Even so, they can still show a level of improvement if they put their mind to it.

The other type of vet is the 'comeback' rider who, until now, may never have trained properly or

scientifically – and he can work wonders.

There was one vet who came back in his late 40s; he immediately launched into a series of enthusiastic questions about new coaching methods, at the end of which he asked 'What time do you think I could do if I took up racing again?'

Now in his previous racing career he had done a 59-minute '25', but at that time he had been short of cash, so he hadn't had the equipment he could afford now. In addition, he was very determined, and had never really lost his basic fitness even though he had not been cycling for some years.

He was astounded and frankly disbelieving when he received the answer that after about a year or 15 months of progressive training he could probably expect a 58-minute ride. 'You're mad!' he replied. 'I've only ever done a '59', and I'll never reach those heights again.'

Yet the following year he did a '57'. It shows how a veteran with the right attitude and plenty of determination can progress. The over-40 has a lot going for him compared with his younger rivals. His career is normally established, and he is more settled and generally better off. He is wiser by years, and can therefore plan to use his time better and analyse the value of training. These factors, combined with better roads and better equipment, should be a spur to any rider aiming to beat his times of a decade or two ago.

Such comeback riders should take stock of themselves before starting a training programme. If you are one of them, then ask yourself: are you grossly overweight or are you still reasonably fit? – and act

accordingly. See your doctor for a check-up, and get his assurance that you are able to tackle a programme of progressive training. Don't frighten him with the idea of cycle racing, because many doctors just don't understand what it entails and they will simply advise against it. But there are a number of factors on which your doctor can advise: your general state of fitness, any physical abnormalities, or whether any past illness might have left its mark.

However, even when you have your doctor's OK, there are other matters to be considered when you are planning your programme, such as your family commitments, your job stress and your other interests.

It is important that your initial programme is not only progressive, but gently progressive. Your early miles should be steady, because as you get older your maximum heart and respiration rates become reduced. This means that hard work on the bike will quickly bring you near your maximum heart rate, which at an early stage is not good. So at first, ride at a pace which won't lift the rate to an uncomfortable level.

The generally-accepted maximum efficient heart rate for a youngster is around 180 beats per minute, but this falls with age. The formula for the maximum rate is to deduct your age from 200, which means that a 40-year-old should regard 160 as his effective maximum, and should keep his pulse below that maximum during training. As you increase your fitness, so your ability to withstand pressure will also increase, and it will take much more work to bring your heart rate up to maximum.

One other factor to consider is

flexibility. This decreases with age, so any veteran training programme must include stretching exercises at least once a day, and carried out gently at first. You won't get the best out of your muscles if they haven't their fully elasticity. You can also improve your strength through gym work or weight training under expert guidance.

But the cornerstone of your early training must be long, steady distance riding. As your fitness improves, mix in speed training and intervals according to need, but only after you have achieved basic fitness. This cannot and must not be rushed.

And if you find training is beginning to pall, try some fartlek training – 'speed play'. Vets can get a lot of enjoyment by going out in a small group and riding as the fancy takes them, perhaps sprinting for signs, ambling along or speeding up as they please.

Be methodical about your approach. Monitor your resting pulse regularly, keep a training diary, and include reports about your feelings generally. Note any feelings of dizziness, chest pains or areas of numbness. Details which you might tend to ignore as a youngster should be examined more carefully if you are a vet. Don't be afraid to go to your doctor.

Women and cycle racing

A lot of the differences between men and women are usually brought about by social and cultural pressures during pre-adolescence and adolescence itself. In recent years these pressures have been decreasing, but they are still a factor.

Nowadays women and girls can do more of the things they want without any social restrictions, and hence many more are coming into sport. This will be a benefit for all sportswomen, because the more they participate, the more and deeper will be the research into the particular problems of women in competition.

As well as the social pressures which sportswomen have to contend with, especially when they are tackling sports which do not have a long tradition of female participation, they also have to deal with the hormonal differences. Men have higher levels of the 'male' hormones such as testosterone, which assist in strength and development. Women have less of this type of hormone, and as a result are at a disadvantage in track events and road sprinting where greater strength is important.

Women have a higher level of oestrogen, which is partly responsible for their having more fat. It is looked upon as 'essential' fat since it is sex-related – as in the breasts, for example. But as women take part in more distance events such as cycle racing and marathon running, their fat levels are being

reduced. It will be interesting to see in the future whether physiologists revise their ideas of just how much of that fat is really 'essential'.

One property of oestrogen is that it blocks the metabolism of fat, and this restricts the use of body fat as an energy source in longer distance races. It is interesting that fat metabolism has actually been improved in some women as a result of long, steady distance work.

Menstruation

The major difference between the male and the female athlete is that the woman has the complication of menstruation. The monthly period affects women in various ways, and it is important for every woman athlete to recognise exactly how it affects her personally, both physically and mentally. It has yet to be shown that competing strenuously during menstruation has a bad effect, so do not assume that an important event will be 'ruined' if it clashes with a period.

Some women find their ability tails off during their period, others actually perform better. It is important for female athletes to know, therefore, just how menstruation affects them personally, and to act accordingly. If you are a racing woman who suffers during her periods, and you are selected for international races, then you should discuss this matter with the federation's doctor, who can advise you on the possible alternatives. There are ways of deferring the menstrual period until after a major event, if required, but this is a matter for planning and medical supervision.

Strenuous exercise can and has affected the regularity of periods. Light training doesn't usually affect them, but exceptionally heavy training can sometimes advance the period or upset its regularity. Any such irregularity corrects itself when training is reduced again. There is no known adverse effect of such irregularities, but they are worth mentioning to the federation doctor or your own GP just in case your racing is not the culprit.

One definite 'plus' of training and racing is the reduction of pre-menstrual tension. Whether this is because of different levels of hormone production, or whether the exercise helps generally, is not known.

There is no reason to suppose that strenuous exercise will affect a woman's fertility, given the numbers of racing women who take a season or two off then come back with an enlarged family in tow.

Pregnancy

Many women have raced successfully during the early stages of pregnancy, but later on it is worth considering the possible adverse effects, especially of crashes – quite apart from the effect of exhaustion on the unborn child.

Training

Women racing cyclists will benefit especially well from their initial long-steady-distance training by improving their ability to metabolise fat, and thus reducing some of their basic body fat. However, like men,

they shouldn't concentrate exclusively on distance training, but should gradually bring in speed and high-intensity work. In the first instance they are at a disadvantage because the female body by its very nature cannot take up as much oxygen as can the male, the amount being something like 20–30 per cent lower. This can be improved with the right type of training, providing that the haemoglobin level is correct. This level is regularly at risk because of the blood loss of menstruation.

America's Connie Carpenter, seen here on the way to winning the 1983 world pursuit championship. Connie also won the gold in the 1984 women's Olympic road race, and owes much of her success to her sporting commitment and regular racing against male riders.

Women are on average smaller than men, with a smaller heart and a smaller heart-stroke; and as a result they have higher pulse rates at rest and under effort. But once again, with progressive overload training, there is no reason why they should not approach and sometimes better the typical male levels.

Particularly in the USA, where the female athlete is readily accepted, women racing against men have found that their performances improve greatly, with a consequent improvement in the performance of American women at world level. There is no reason why all racing women shouldn't seek to benefit in the same way; for by racing in the usually tougher company of men they can more easily recognise their own strengths and weaknesses in relation to future international competition. Many top racing women are hardly extended

Britain's Mandy Jones, world road champion in 1982, here seen dominating a woman's road race early in 1983. Her success stemmed from a tough basic training programme which all but ignored the fact that she was a woman.

in the average domestic road race, and only find out their true value when they come up against overseas opposition.

Many women are afraid that training will make them too muscular, but in fact their lower levels of testosterone mean that they can happily launch into weight training or hard cycle training without worrying about developing bulky muscles. Another worry with new women cyclists is that they will get great big bottoms! In fact the opposite is likely to be the case, since cycling helps to pare away the fat pads around the buttocks.

In theory, because women's events are generally shorter than the average men's events, they can get away with fewer training miles a each session; but on the other hand the long-steady-distance sessions help to reduce their body fat, as mentioned earlier.

Because of their physical differences and smaller body frame, racing women can generally use narrower handlebars (typically 38cm wide); but women are generally more comfortable with a wider saddle because of their wider pelvic structure. Many women suffer from soreness around the pubic area, but it is possible to minimise discomfort by wearing a really good-quality chamois shorts insert, and by lubricating the insert with Cetavlex or similar creams.

If you are a woman or girl contemplating training and racing, the important thing to remember is that you are a potential athlete who happens to be female. The principles of training are just the same as with men. The racing woman will not normally be expected to hurt herself as much when she trains; but that is an allowance that men tend to make for women, and women should not make it for themselves. They should go for progressive training in the same way as men do, and not accept any suggeston that they should take an easier path. It is the application of athletic standards rather than traditional female ones that has brought about the success of Beryl Burton and, more recently, Mandy Jones and Connie Carpenter. All three have followed training programmes which would have daunted all but the most dedicated man. And they have come out with world titles because of it. A more powerful lesson could not be learned.

Hitting peak form

The ability to hit peak form at the right moment – 'peaking' – is the ultimate in self-knowledge: a combination of your own self-knowledge with the judgement of your coach.

In general, the foundations of your fitness decide how near you can get to your true potential. Your genetic background, your ability to train, your mental attitudes, your determination: all knit together to make you the kind of rider you eventually become.

When you get to high levels of training, it is easy to do too much and overtrain, with all the attendant problems. So it is vital to heed your body signs and act upon them.

Most roadmen adopt a training programme based firmly on long steady distance and sharpened through speed and high-intensity work. But once their training is in full swing, they tend to look to a stage race in order to give them some further improvement. The stress brought on by competition – day in, day out – is what gives you that racing 'edge'. Of course, you need to recover from the stage race, and this is the point where you are liable to overtrain if you start overloading yourself.

Now you should have your eye on the target race – the 'peak'. The idea is to achieve progressive improvements in your level of effort, interspersed with periods of lesser effort to help you recover and consolidate at the new level. You also need speed work to 'sharpen the edge'.

Your efforts must be geared to

the big race, but tempered by your level of experience in the sport. For example, you cannot expect to move from local events to national events and then on to international stage races in quick succession. There is no point in setting your sights unreasonably high and then suffering the inevitable psychological setback when you do not do well in an event where you never really stood any chance.

So ride your stage race to develop your endurance and racing edge; but follow this with a recovery period of lesser training, until you are sure from your body signs that you are ready to start the climb towards the peak again.

Then tackle a succession of races with the idea of promoting a greater level of fitness. Where you finish isn't really important: it's nice if you can finish well up, but the essential is to have a good work-out. All the while you are listening to your body, watching the progress of your pulse and your weight, noting your sleep patterns. If everything is fine, then progress to still harder training. Provided that you are feeling good, and you're sleeping and eating well, then you should continue with the progressive overload. During the final week you should cut out all endurance work and concentrate on short, sharp work with plenty of rest, so that you get to the start-line full of zip.

Peaking for time trials is different: you don't need stage races to increase your endurance; you are simply looking for speed.

Alf Engers, in preparing for his national-competition 25-mile record ride, was training for speed all the time. He would do a 20-mile ride flat out, followed by a 25-mile two-up session and a flat-out '10'; then a two-up '10', sometimes twice a day; then a five-mile ride against the watch, followed by a five-mile two-up twice a day. He was going for speed all the time, so that in 25-mile events he had an optimum speed very much greater than that of his rivals. His body chemistry was used to speeds much higher than that necessary for the '25', so he was able to handle the necessary speed a lot more easily.

On the track you should look for a series of build-up events that will give you a good physical work-out with little mental stress. Track leagues are ideal for this. Track events produce much greater mental stresses than road events in comparison to the physical stresses involved. So quite often it is mental stress, rather than a strict inability to go fast, that makes a track rider lose his edge.

In pursuiting, it is impossible to build up through pursuiting itself, because the concentration required is too killing. Better to build up through fast road racing – the formula adopted by the British team pursuit squad when they were carrying off medal after medal. Racing on the road in the right kind of event gave them a good foundation of stamina without blunting their speed.

Towards the national pursuit championship, you should cut down on long road races, introducing more criteriums on short circuits, plus some short time trials – and finally track league events to brush up your speed. Throughout this programme you should monitor your body signs for indications that you are starting to do too much too fast.

Recognise the way you feel

The more you train, the more you will grow to recognise the messages that your body is sending out. Try to analyse every training ride and every race. Be honest with yourself, and compare each effort with the goal. In this way you will hopefully know when you are ready to do a 'ride' – to pull off a big win. It's that feeling of firing on all cylinders. Some riders call it 'pinging'.

Don't kid yourself. Telling yourself that you are ready when in fact you are only approaching peak fitness is only inviting disappointment. You can give yourself a real boost by recognising the day when you are ready to perform at your best level, when you are really due for a victory.

If you feel you are fit, but not quite ready for the big one, then acknowledge the fact and set out to use the event as a productive training session.

This self-knowledge is very important for international riders. Riding as part of a team, you will need to speak honestly about your chances; for if it is really 'not your day', then you will do better to sacrifice your own chances by riding as a domestique for a team-mate who is on form.

The hour-a-day fitness programme

Parkinson's Law insists that work expands to fit the time available, and not every reader will be able to spend as much time training as we would recommend. So now is the time to talk about that elusive animal, the training short cut. Follow this as your regular regime, if you like; or preferably only have recourse to it when business, personal or domestic commitments eat into your normal training time. What do you do if you only have an hour to train? The answer is to try to substitute quality for quantity.

This system is one of progressive overload, and goes through six distinct stages, each one lasting a theoretical two weeks. It presupposes that you have plenty of long-steady-distance work behind you, and are therefore basically fit.

You might wonder why you shouldn't just do this kind of training anyway, since it clearly uses up less time. The answer is that this shortened programme is not for everyone. It is physically possible for everyone, but some riders cannot come to terms with the mental demands it places on you. Above all, it requires a commitment from the outset that you will strive to do the programme to its fullest. There are no short cuts with this short cut!

Although we have indicated that each phase should last two weeks, you can vary it if you feel that a move into the next phase is premature. Don't seek to move as

Phase one

Period to last **2** weeks

Monday to Friday
Sessions to be taken alone
Speed **20 mph**
Gear **medium/high**
Duration **1 hour**

Saturdays
Alone or in company
Speed **20 mph**
Gear **medium/high**
Duration **1 hour**

Sunday(s)
Race

Note:
1. Before every session you will need to warm up for approximately 10–15 minutes, and each session should be concluded with a warm-down.
2. Record daily pulse rate night and morning.
3. Record your weight weekly and note changes.

Phase two

Period to last **2** weeks

Monday to Friday
Sessions to be taken alone
Speed **20 mph**
Gear **medium/high**
Duration **1 hour**

Introduce 8 sprints of 150 metres, split evenly during the session. Sessions should end with a 2½-mile time trial at 90–95% effort. Conclude with a warm-down.

Saturday
Alone or in company
Speed **20 mph**
Gear **medium**
Duration **1 hour**

Sunday
Race

Note:
1. Before every session you will need to warm up for approximately 10–15 minutes, and each session should be concluded with a warm-down.
2. Record daily pulse rate night and morning.
3. Record your weight weekly and note changes.

Phase three

Period to last **2** weeks

Monday to Friday
Sessions to be taken alone or in company
Speed **20 mph**
Gear **medium/high**
Duration **1 hour**

You should now introduce sprints up to a total of 15 over 200 metres. Finish each session with a 3½-mile time trial at 90–95% effort. Conclude with a warm-down.

Saturday
Alone or in company
Speed **20 mph**
Gear **medium**
Duration **1 hour**

Sunday
Race

Note:
1. Before every session you will need to warm up for approximately 10–15 minutes, and each session should be concluded with a warm-down.
2. Record daily pulse rate night and morning.
3. Record your weight weekly and note changes.

Phase four

Period to last _2_ weeks

Monday to Friday
Sessions to be taken alone or in company
Speed _20 mph_
Gear _medium/high_
Duration _1 hour_

You should now include sprints to a total of 23 over 250 metres. Finish each session with a 5-mile time trial at 90–95% effort.

Saturday
Race

Sunday
Race

Notes:
1. Before every session you must warm up for approximately 10–15 minutes, and each session should be concluded with a warm-down.
2. Record your pulse rate night and morning.
3. Record your weight weekly and note changes.

Phase five

Period to last _2_ weeks

Monday
Rest day or low-gear recovery ride.

Tuesday
Interval sprints alone as in phase four.

Wednesday
Individual time trial of approximately 22 miles, using high gears, at 95% effort. Work on your riding style.

Thursday
Interval sprints alone as in phase two.

Friday
Interval sprints, as in phase four – varying between 150 and 300 metres uphill, downhill, on the flat, and in and out of bends. Balance the sprints to cover all areas equally. Finish with a 6–7½-mile time trial.

Saturday
Steady ride of 1 hour's duration at fairly low gears. Enjoy it.

Sunday
Race or simulated race.

Notes:
Record changes in your condition, weight, mental awareness and pulse rate; note any overtiredness.

Phase six

Period to last _2_ weeks

Monday
Rest day or low-gear recovery ride.

Tuesday
Interval sprints as in phase four – at least 30 sprints, varying between 120 and 300 metres, uphill, downhill, on the flat, and in and out of bends. Balance the sprints to cover all areas equally. Finish with a 6–7½-mile time trial.

Wednesday
Company ride – simulated race. Conditions and tactics, echelons, sprints, etc. Learn about your colleagues' strengths and weaknesses and exploit them.

Thursday
As in phase three (Monday–Friday).

Friday
As in phase four (Monday–Friday).

Saturday
Steady ride of 1 hour's duration at fairly low gears. Enjoy it.

Sunday
Race day.

Notes:
Record changes in your condition, weight, mental awareness and pulse rate; note any overtiredness.

rapidly as possible through each phase, but move on to the next one only when you sense you have mastered the challenge of the one in hand.

Most people are fit enough to tackle phase one. It is indicated for two weeks, but it can last six weeks or one week, according to need.

Phase two is of greater intensity. Here again, you must only move on when you are on top of this phase – when you find you are extended, but not completely 'smashed'.

As you move through phases three, four, five and six, the training gets harder and harder. It is important to watch your body signs and heed what they tell you; for although you will only be training for

an hour, the training is hard and progressively increases in intensity. If you ignore your body signs, and proceed through the phases too fast, you will find you have done too much. If you follow through at the right rate for your body, you will be very fit and on top of your training.

If you already have basic fitness, then you can economise on the subsequent training time. A good example of this was the case of Ian Hallam, who had many international honours on road and track. While he was studying at the School of Dentistry he had only an hour a day in which to train. He used it on interval training, and carried on winning events at top level against riders who were training for much longer than he was.

If you are training for longer events and stage races, then you must put in more hours in the saddle. The six-phase programme won't give you that kind of high-level endurance. But for shorter and average distance events it can give you a very good state of fitness indeed.

But a lot of people are not inclined to put in a real effort. Many just do the same training week in, week out, with no element of progressive overload. So they simply don't progress. The six-phase programme requires physical and mental concentration if it is to succeed. So you must first decide if you are of the right calibre to tackle it and benefit.

Body fuel

When people talk about 'diets' it is usually in the sense of cutting out something. So when thinking about diet for sport, it is better to substitute the word *nutrition* – eating food that does you good.

There are no wonder foods that will make you a super-champion. Neither will your form disappear overnight if you sample some 'forbidden fruit'. But if you are a cyclist devoting a lot of time to your sport, then it is logical to give your body the best chance of benefitting from the training and competition it receives, by keeping it well supplied with the right kind of food.

The average spare-time sportsman will not go far wrong if he follows the traditional 'balanced diet' which is happily the norm in Britain, America and most of Europe, where meat, vegetables, cereals and dairy foods are readily available.

But the more work you do, the more any deficiencies in your normal way of feeding are likely to betray you. So it is better to make an effort to understand what your body needs, and to cater for this,

with a specific dietary regime.

There is much argument over the supplementation of a normal healthy regime with extra vitamins and minerals. Doctors will usually tell you that you are highly unlikely to be deficient if you follow healthy eating rules. This, however, presupposes that you are not laid low by illness, injury or shock, that you don't sweat overmuch, and that you don't extend yourself greatly over a long period. No cyclist can afford to make that kind of assumption. Since any of these circumstances leads to an abnormal demand for the body's vital substances, there must be occasions when balanced supplementation is indicated.

There are certainly medical conditions in which very large doses of vitamins are prescribed, but this should be the subject of expert supervision only. It is possible to overdose on some vitamins – namely A, D, E and K – because they are fat-soluble, and therefore cannot be carried out of the system in the urine. The water-soluble vitamins B and C can be removed this way when taken to excess, and therefore cannot harm the body.

It will certainly do you no harm to take a balanced multi-vitamin supplement, and these can be

bought over the counter at any chemist. For much of the time you won't run any risk of deficiency, thanks to a normal diet and normal training/racing. But there may be occasions when your stores of vitamins and minerals will dip – and this is when you will need the extra 'insurance' of the multi-vitamin tablet.

In addition, there will be times when certain vitamins are recommended to be taken for certain circumstances, and these are mentioned elsewhere in the book.

Your regime has to take care of various demands the body makes for:

1. Energy
2. Growth and repair
3. Regulating body processes

These are satisfied in the following ways:

1. *Energy:* from carbohydrates, fats and proteins

2. *Growth and repair:* by means of proteins, trace elements and water

3. *Regulating the body processes:* by means of vitamins, trace elements, water, and certain proteins

Energy sources

For the cyclist, carbohydrates are the most efficient energy source. Carbohydrates are broken down into glucose, which is ready for action in the muscles in the form of glycogen. Further glycogen is stored in the liver, and any excess is stored in the tissues as body fat. Typical carbohydrate sources are honey, glucose, potatoes, bread, rice and pasta.

Fats have a higher energy rating, but they are not so easily broken down for use as energy fuel. Never take a lot of fats as part of a pre-race meal. Any excess of fats automatically becomes body fat.

Protein is also an energy source, but a poor one. The body calls upon it only when all other energy sources are exhausted.

Nutrients concerned with growth and repair

Proteins (From the Greek word meaning 'of first importance')	For growth and repair of the body cells, muscle tissues, etc.	*1st Class:* Whole milk, meat, cheese, eggs, fish *2nd Class:* Beans, peas, corn, bread, soya beans, dry non-fat milk
Calcium, Phosphorus, Magnesium	Formation and maintenance of bones and teeth	Milk, cheese, eggs, sardines, meat, wholegrain cereals, green vegetables, bread, herring
Iron, Phosphorus	Formation and repair of body cells, red corpuscles, liver, muscles	Liver, wholemeal bread, peas, cheese, cereal, fish, cabbage, potatoes
Sulphur	Formation and repair of body cells, red corpuscles, liver, muscles	Available in all protein foods
Sodium chloride	Formation and maintenance of body fluids (i.e. intracellular and intravascular fluids)	Table salt, animal sea foods, abundant in most foods except fruit
Potassium	Formation and maintenance of body fluids (i.e. intracellular and intravascular fluids)	Fruit, milk, meat, cereals, vegetables
Water	Formation and maintenance of body fluids and body cells	Most foods contain large amounts of water, plus what is drunk

Nutrients regulating body processes

Phosphorus, Manganese, Copper, Iron	The complex processes by which the body obtains energy from food; efficient oxygenation of the blood	Liver, meat, bread, egg yolk, cheese, peanuts, some sea foods, green vegetables
Iodine	Part of a substance in the thyroid gland regulating the release of energy	Sea foods; vegetables grown in areas where soil contains iodine; iodised table salt
Calcium	Part of the processes involved in blood clotting; muscle function	Milk, cheese, dark green leafy vegetables, sardines, herring, bread
Water	Regulation of body temperature through sweating	Most foods, plus normal liquid intake
Some proteins	Form part of the digestive enzymes	Milk, cheese, meat, fish, eggs

Vitamins

Vitamins are vital to the regulation of the body processes, and their deficiency can have startling results. When watching your intake of vitamins, bear in mind that they are lost in cooking or storage; so try to eat food fresh and, wherever possible and palatable, raw. It is also a healthy move to go where possible for whole foods – i.e. those without additives and with none of the goodness taken out. In this way you should be sure of a regular vitamin and mineral supply.

Here are the vitamins in detail, together with their functions, sources and (most important) some of the substances which reduce their effect:

Vitamin A (Carotene) – fat-soluble
Promotes skin health
Helps resistance to infection
Helps bones develop
Maintains good eyesight
Sources: melon, peach, carrot, lettuce, broccoli, parsley, fish-liver oils, butter, margarine, offal, certain nuts
Depleting factors: cortisone and other drugs, excess alcohol, iron consumption, coffee, tobacco

Vitamin B Complex – water-soluble

B1 (Thiamine)
Carbohydrate metabolism
Energy production
Growth, appetite, digestion
Nerve activity
Gastro-intestinal tonus
Sources: wheatgerm, soya-bean flour, brewers' yeast, beans, potatoes, cereals, nuts, some fish
Depleting factors: alcohol, antibiotics, birth-control pills, coffee, stress, diarrhoea (N.B. increase intake when increasing intake of carbohydrate)

B2 (Riboflavin)
Maintains skin, digestive tract and vision
Co-enzyme in respiratory enzyme system
Sources: offal, avocado, soya beans, nuts, cheese, milk, potatoes, cereal
Depleting factors: alcohol, birth-control pills, tobacco, coffee

B3 (Niacin)
Circulation system
Growth
Maintenance of nervous system
Co-enzyme in tissue respiration and fat synthesis
Sources: meat, fish, peanuts, brewers' yeast
Depleting factors: alcohol, antibiotics, birth-control pills, coffee, corn, tissue trauma

B5 (Pantothenic acid)
Antibody formation
Carbohydrate metabolism
Stimulation of adrenals
Keeps skin and nerves healthy
Sources: liver, spinach, broccoli, eggs, milk
Depleting factors: alcohol, coffee, sleeping pills, stress

B6 (Pyridoxine)
Co-enzyme in protein, fat and carbohydrate metabolism
Controls magnesium levels
Sources: liver, herring, potatoes, pork, whole-grain cereals, eggs, milk
Depleting factors: ageing, alcohol, sleeping pills, radiation exposure, birth-control pills

B12 (Cyanocobalamin)
Co-enzyme in protein synthesis
Blood cell formation
Maintenance of nerve tissue
Sources: offal, egg yolk, cheese, milk, fish, meat
Depleting factors: ageing, alcohol, coffee, laxatives, sleeping pills

B15 (Pangamic acid)
This is a 'disputed' vitamin, whose reputation is the subject of unresolved arguments. However, the Russians have claimed to use it to benefit athletes.
Cell oxydation and respiration
Increases the body's efficiency in using oxygen
Stimulates glucose, fat and protein metabolism
Sources: no natural usable sources, so available only in tablet form
Depleting factors: alcohol, birth-control pills, coffee, sleeping pills

Vitamin C (Ascorbic acid) – water-soluble
Absorption of iron
Calcium diffusion
Synthesis of collagen
Maintenance of blood vessels
Sources: citrus fruits, blackcurrants, rose-hips, cabbage, brussels sprouts, tomatoes, potatoes
Depleting factors: antibiotics, anxiety, aspirin, burns, cortisone, sulfa drugs, tobacco, stress

Vitamin D (Calciferol) – fat-soluble
Normal growth through bone growth
Absorption of calcium and phosphorus
Gland and nerve function
Sources: tuna, halibut- and cod-liver oils, herring, sardines, butter, margarine, milk, eggs, sunlight
Depleting factors: mineral oils

Vitamin E (Tocopherol) – fat-soluble
Normal growth maintenance
Normal muscle metabolism
Maintains integrity of central nervous system and circulation
Maintains kidney tubules, lungs, genital structures and liver
Sources: lettuce, corn, green peppers, peanuts, wheatgerm, whole-wheat flour
Depleting factors: air pollution, birth-control pills, iron

Vitamin K (Menadione) – fat-soluble
Normal blood clotting
Normal liver function
Sources: cabbage, cauliflower, soya beans, pork, beef, liver, potatoes, tomatoes, egg yolk
Depleting factors: air pollution, antibiotics, aspirin, diarrhoea

On the subject of this list, here is one word of warning: don't monkey about with your vitamin and mineral intake. The aim in nutrition is to have a sufficiency, not an excess. Just because a substance aids the formation of muscle, for instance, it does not follow that megadosing will form lots of muscle; it might form lots of problems instead. Balance is the keynote, which is why sticking to balanced multi-vitamin supplements is the only safe way of taking extra vitamins.

So don't make any great departures from the traditional balanced diet, but at the same time be on the look-out for any signs of deficiency. If you know what the various vitamins do, you may then be able to identify deficiency as the cause of a problem. If you suspect that you have some deficiency, then check this out with someone qualified. Don't take matters into your own hands.

Protein and fats are easy to get in a normal diet, so don't concentrate on increasing your intake. In fact, you can generally cut out some of the fats in your regime. The key substance for hard-working cyclists is carbohydrate. So next time you sit down to a plate of steak and rice, reflect that you may need the rice more than the steak!

Carbohydrate loading

When it was first introduced to the athletic world, the idea of carbohydrate loading caused quite a stir of interest.

Now that so many people are trying it, some disadvantages have become apparent. Depriving your body of glycogen can upset you, and there is a danger of unwanted fluid retention when you load carbohydrates, which can also be upsetting in its way.

We have found that a modified version of carbo-loading can be used more frequently and with few side-effects. However, for the sake of comparison, here is the original method.

From the sixth to the fourth day prior to the chosen event, you would concentrate your diet on protein and fat: meat, fish, poultry, eggs and so on. Carbohydrate intake would thus be limited. You would be training well and hard throughout this period, which would bring about an exhaustion or lowering of your stores of natural blood glucose, and of glycogen in your liver. You would make sure of this by putting in a really tough training session at the end of this period.

For the next three days leading up to the race, you would eat several meals which were very rich in carbohydrate, thus forcing the muscles to hold a higher level of glucose than they would accept with a normal diet – which of course would give you a better store of ready energy.

This has had its disadvantages. One of the problems of eating a surfeit of carbohydrate is that you tend to retain a lot of body fluid. If body fluid is retained in the muscles, it is also retained in the cardiac (heart) muscle. This affects the efficiency of the heart and brings about a lowering of the performance level or, in an unfit person, an element of actual danger.

This is why cyclists experimenting under guidance with carbo-loading have found the modified method more effective. That is, to follow a regular diet for the first three days, to avoid the tough, glucose-depleting training session at the end of the period, and simply to increase carbohydrate intake considerably over the final three days. Some riders can suffer potassium deficiency during the carbo-loading phase. Avoid this by taking a couple of good glasses of fruit juice each day.

Race food

As with any food and drink, you can exercise your own personal preferences, but within certain guidelines.

Your last big meal should be at least three hours before the start of the race, and will often be dinner the night before. It should contain plenty of carbohydrate, which will be your energy source for the race.

If there is an early start, as usually happens with time trials, all you need is a light breakfast to take up the acid in your stomach, for example toast and honey and a drink to your taste. But nothing highly sugary in great quantities. Instead of providing your body with energy, as you might expect, a sudden influx of sugar will usually have the opposite effect: your blood-sugar level will drop, and you will feel sluggish because of the insulin imbalance.

During the race itself, you need to replace your lost body fluids by means of electrolyte replacement drinks. Wander's Mineral Plus-6 is good, as are all the foods produced by Wander. Staminade, Gatorade and XL-1 all fall in this particular group. These drinks replace the mineral salts lost in sweat, usually with added glucose, ostensibly to top up energy sources. However, do try these drinks out beforehand on training rides: they don't suit everyone's stomach, and they just might upset you. Alternative drinks are plain water, weak tea (without milk), lemon tea, and cola syrup with water to taste.

Race feeding depends basically on the duration of the race: you can

Above: A sensible way to take a drink during a road race. This rider takes a quiet swig from his bottle while lying slightly off the back of the group and out of their sight.

Right: Events over dusty roads bring problems of gritty eyes and irritated throats.

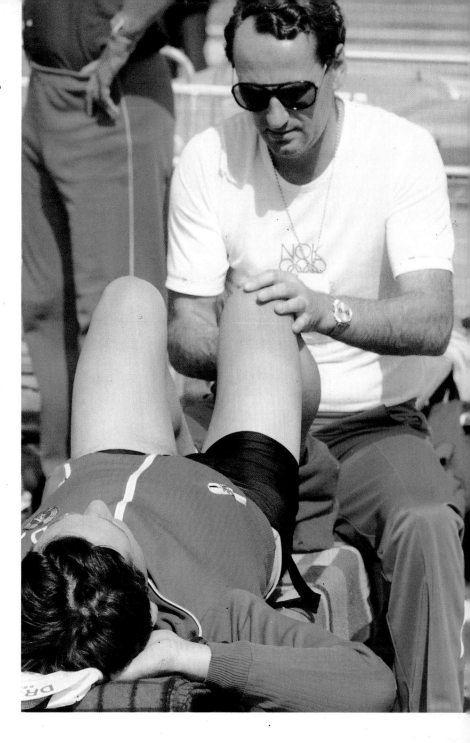

Left: A watersplash during the Milk Race—an unexpected occurrence for the riders, and possibly an unwelcome one. Sudden exposure to cold water can produce muscle cramps.

Right: Massage for a trackman in between races. This kind of massage must be brisk and stimulating.

The positive face of cycle racing. Australia's Phil Anderson looks really determined. Having come halfway across the world to make his fortune in cycle racing, such a rider is not likely to have the 'flight' reaction in a tough moment.

Handing up a musette of food during a long road event. Normally enough food and drink can be carried for events up to 100 miles.

go anything up to 80 kilometres without taking anything at all, because you will still be drawing on the energy from pre-race meals.

For events of longer duration you can use Wander Energy Bars (which are very good), Plus-Food drink (which needs to be sipped, because it is the equivalent of a meal), Kendal Mint Cake or

glucose. However, glucose does tend to dehydrate you, so should be used only sparingly as a quick energy source. Fruit cake, malt loaf with honey, bridge rolls with a slice of peach inside, and miniature apple pies, are all good energy sources.

The aim is to take up the acids in the stomach and also steadily to restock the energy lost. Better to start eating early in the race – eating little and often – than to have to start stuffing glucose down your throat as an emergency measure.

On one occasion during the Milk Race, Bob Downs had a very bad attack of food poisoning and spent

several nights going to and from the toilet; but thanks to a high-energy-replacement drink called Wander Power-Back, he was able to keep going and later to become useful again as a team member.

Liquid protein drinks don't really have any place in race feeding, because in the western world we don't have a protein problem. If anything we tend to eat too much protein. The idea that throwing down a lot of protein will make you a big bundle of muscle has no foundation.

Beware of how you mix your foods. Some foods mix well with others, while certain types of food should be eaten alone or with others of the same food group. The groups are listed on the next page. Carbohydrates normally go through the system much faster than proteins and fats, which require between three and five hours for digestion. But when concentrated carbohydrates are eaten together with protein and fat, they are simply trapped in the stomach. The sugars then combine with the various digestive juices to create fermentation. This in turn produces gas, which has to come out at one end or the other. The development and removal of gas from the digestive system takes up body energy; so prior to competition, it can be a waste of energy (as well as an embarrassment) to mix carbohydrates with the two other groups of food.

How foods combine (or not)

**Concentrated carbohydrates
(eat these on their own)**

Proteins and/or fats

Combinations

Cakes Pastries Sweet drinks Fruit juices Fruit Sweets and chocolate White bread	}	*Do not mix well – if mixed, produce body gases*	Meat Fish Eggs Dairy produce Protein drinks	}	*Good mix*	Vegetables Whole-grain bread Cereals

130

9 *Looking after yourself*

Staying healthy

Looking good

Appearance is very important in bike-riding. You are bound to come into contact with members of the public; and if you are a dirty, scruffy rider on a dirty, scruffy bike, then you won't make a good impression and the sport won't either. Professional riders and top amateurs are always smart.

It doesn't cost a lot to be clean, or to keep your bike clean. If you regularly clean your bike then you stand a good chance of avoiding mechanical troubles, because you will quickly spot problems in the making, such as frayed cables, a nick in the tyre, even a cracked crank or frame tube.

A lot of the 'bad luck' experienced during racing is just a matter of bad bike preparation. The puncture at the wrong moment might have come from a flint in the tyre that could have been removed during a regular cleaning session. A broken toe-clip might have been spotted too. You can make your own luck.

It's not just a question of having

Professional cycling is a business. Former world pursuit champion Tony Doyle looks every inch the businessman.

Clean and neat before the start of an event, professional John Herety signs an autograph.

the best equipment. Whatever equipment and clothing you have, there is no excuse for not keeping it clean. And if you look good, you feel good – and as a result you train and race better.

Work at good health

You can't take it for granted that you will automatically enjoy good health. You have to work at it. So during the off-season take the opportunity for a medical check-up and a visit to the dentist. Clean your teeth at least twice a day. You should also have a course of prophylactic anti-tetanus injections. If you have a crash during the season, the chances are you will be given a jab anyway, unless you have already had a course. Better to suffer a few weeks off form during the winter than at the height of the season. When you go to races, put your proof of anti-tetanus inside your racing licence.

Keeping your body clean will guard against skin problems, especially in the sensitive area of the crutch. You will minimise the danger of pimples, spots and boils developing as a result of chafing and consequent irritation of the follicles.

Clothes used for training shouldn't be donned again until they have been washed, since the sweat they absorb will harbour infective bacteria and create painful and embarrassing skin problems. At this point it is worth mentioning the use of biological washing powders. If you use them to wash racing and training clothing, make sure they are very well rinsed; otherwise some of the enzymes will stay on the clothes and will react with the sweat to produce a skin rash.

Keeping your fingernails short and clean also helps to avoid skin problems. If you start scratching yourself with dirty fingernails, you are inviting skin trouble.

Another area of personal hygiene which is often neglected is that of the feet. Lots of riders don't bother to have a regular good look at their feet, yet this is one of the areas that takes a lot of pounding as a result of cycling. Nails should be trimmed regularly, and cut straight across, not rounded; otherwise you risk an ingrowing toenail. If you do get one, a small 'V' cut in the centre of the

nail can help to gradually draw it out from the edges and relieve the pain. You should wash your feet regularly and always wear clean socks. Apply cream or powder, depending on whether your feet tend to be excessively dry or excessively sweaty. Menthol cream or talcum powder is recommended.

When you get back from training, have a wash-down as quickly as possible, and change into warm clothes. Don't stand around in wet clothes. Always take a nylon racing cape or jacket in your back pocket as an insurance against the weather turning very bad.

Another tip if you are going to ride into a strong chilling wind: between two jerseys put a layer of plastic blister packing – the type with air bubbles. This is sold in various widths and can be trimmed to form an apron. As a reserve, find a Japanese-made product used as a heat source by fishermen. It is a plastic bag of granules which produce heat when activated. It's like having a hot water bottle at your disposal when and where you need it. One day you will be caught out on the moors in inclement weather, and you will be pleased to have it along.

Your eyes need regular care. They can get very sore, especially in rain or wind. Try not to rub them, especially with gritty fingers or – even worse – fingers covered with embrocation (which can be dangerous). If you do come in from a windy or dusty ride, use an eye-bath and solution. Bear in mind that these solutions have a very short life once opened, so they need to be bought in small quantities and frequently. If you have any unusual problems with your eyes, go to see your optician.

Some people get problems with a build-up of wax in the ears. Resist the temptation to attack the wax with matchsticks or anything else. It is surprising how easily your ears can be damaged. Far better to visit your doctor for some softening drops or to have your ears syringed out.

Sex and racing

Yes, they do mix! The fitter you are, the better your sexual functions are likely to be. If you are unfit, you are unable to perform the sexual act as well as you would otherwise.

Sex before racing – the night before – poses no problems providing that sex occupies a regular part of your life. If you normally have sex every day, then abstaining just because of a race the following day will do you no good at all.

One notable rider some time ago decided that sex was draining his strength, so on the build-up to a big event he resolved to sleep apart from his wife. Nature had its way, however, and on the night before the race he had a nocturnal emission – a 'wet dream' – and as a result his confidence was completely drained. He would have done better to have continued his normal loving relationship with his wife.

If you don't have a regular sexual relationship, then it's a different story: the hours of sleep lost when out looking for sex are just as detrimental as the 'effort' itself.

Travelling positively

If you are going to be any good at cycle racing, you can expect at some point to be invited to race overseas. Travel can adversely affect performance, especially when it involves time-zone changes. So it's in your interests to try to minimise the adverse effects of travelling, especially to somewhere new, in as many ways as possible. Start by learning about the country concerned: the weather conditions, the terrain, the local food and customs. If you know what differences to expect, then the resulting stress will be greatly lessened.

The effect of 'jet lag' is also a problem. It upsets your body rhythms, your biological clock and probably your digestion. You wake up and go to sleep at the wrong time. Unless you have plenty of time to adapt, your body will not function efficiently.

Minimising the effects of jet-lag is achieved by a few easy precautions. First of all, don't get in

British professionals relax before the start of a sunny event: (left to right) Graham Jones, John Herety, Steve Jones.

a lot of miles immediately before departure, so you don't start the trip in an exhausted state. A missed day of training is a small price to pay for arriving in a much better condition. When you get on the plane, adjust your watch to the local time of your destination. In this way you are already starting to adjust to the new venue. Think of your day and night patterns immediately in terms of your destination. As far as you can, start to eat and sleep as if you were already in the new time zone.

When eating, remember that for the first half of the day you should be having more protein, and in the second half you should have more carbohydrate. On the plane, if it's breakfast time at your destination, select items which have more protein, then as the day goes on alter to take in more carbohydrate. Don't eat a lot, but drink plenty of non-alcoholic fluids. Try to sleep on the plane. Take some slippers, and wear loose clothing so your circulation is unrestricted. Have a walk around the cabin from time to time to give your heart some work, or do some easy isometric exercises in your seat.

When you arrive, go for a gentle ride to assess the conditions and get your bearings. If you are at the world championships, for instance, don't get caught up in a fast-moving training group of international stars if you visit the course. Far better to gently reconnoitre the course, and to concentrate on recovering from the journey.

Extreme conditions

It would be nice if all racing and training were carried out in ideal conditions, but we don't live in an ideal world. So you need to know what precautions to take in extremes of weather.

Hot weather
First of all, avoid foods that are going to push up your body temperature, particularly chocolate.

You need plenty of fluids to replace the loss in sweat. These should preferably be in the form of electrolyte replacement drinks designed to replace body fluids in a balanced manner. Don't take salt tablets except in extreme conditions and under medical supervision.

Clothing should be loose-fitting to allow the air to flow through, and you should protect your neck and the tender parts of the upper arms with sun-barrier cream. And wear a hat, of course, with the peak back or forward according to your needs. If you don't have a sun-tan and come to race in a hot climate, then use a barrier cream with the appropriate strength factor.

Dehydration is the major danger, closely followed by heat exhaustion. Signs of this are dizziness, headache and lack of co-ordination. If you notice these symptoms, get off your bike and sit in the shade until help arrives.

Cold weather
You can take warm foods and drinks in a thermos flask which fits your bottle cage, or in a thermic bottle, or in a thermos refill fitted into the bottom half of a normal feeding bottle. A warm drink at the right time is a great advantage.

You need to eat more because of the extra calories used in actually keeping warm. Here the proverbial Mars bar or other type of chocolate comes in handy.

Just because you are racing, it doesn't mean you should be in a short-sleeved jersey and skinshorts whatever the temperature. If it's cold, don't be afraid to don training tights, extra jerseys, gloves, hat and overshoes. You can also put warming embrocation on the knees – an oil-based one if the conditions are wet.

Danger signs in the cold are numbness and shivering, and a tightening of the stomach. Frostbite in the fingers is not totally unknown. If you suspect frostbite, then carefully restore warmth to the threatened fingers or toes, but only very gradually. Don't rub them. Put them in your pockets or warm them under your armpits.

High altitude
If you go straight into racing at high altitude it can be a traumatic experience, because the body's ability to breathe normally is impaired. You need a period of at least three weeks at altitude to acclimatise properly, but one helping factor is high dosage of vitamin E – about 1000mg daily, but only under close supervision. Altitude also brings the problem of dehydration, so look once more to your fluid intake.

Also watch your pulse rate, which will go very high at first. Start taking 200mg of vitamin E daily until your pulse stabilises, then move up to the higher dosage.

If you are taking medication, especially sleeping tablets, watch for increased effectiveness and dose accordingly.

Racing in cold weather means dressing sensibly. Long sleeves, training tights, gloves and overshoes are well in evidence here.

Fatigue and overtraining

Resting actively

Work hard at getting the rest you will need, especially during a period of heavy racing, and most of all during a stage race. The old saying of 'Don't stand when you can sit, don't sit when you can lie' is most appropriate.

Sleep is of utmost importance for recovery in time for the next day. Sleep requirements vary from one individual to another, but you can work out your normal requirement by a simple experiment. When time permits, and when you are not racing or doing anything else important, go to bed at your normal time and sleep until you wake up naturally. Do this over a period of a week and you will have a fair idea of the average time you need to sleep. Once you know your sleep requirement, adjust your retiring time to give you the right sleep period before an event the following day.

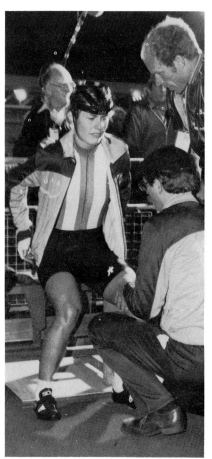

Getting in every moment of rest and recuperation between heats – American woman sprinter Connie Paraskevin.

The danger signs

If you feel unaccountably weary, it could be that you are overtraining. Of course training should make you feel tired, but recovery should be accomplished virtually overnight, and certainly the next day. Your resting pulse rate is the clearest indication.

Extreme fatigue brings unmistakable signs: altered sleep patterns, loss of appetite and a feeling of no energy, general muscle weakness. This usually comes about through a combination of high mileage and high-intensity work. You have simply overloaded yourself with training.

This is a difficult and highly complex situation. Normally you need to train to help you recover faster. The faster your recovery, the more you can train. The more you can train, the better your fitness. The better your fitness, the harder you can train. The harder you can train, the faster your recovery. In a perfect world, this is a recipe for reaching the top; but you have to reckon with influences outside your normal training routine which can overbalance it.

There are domestic factors – school, work, home, finances – which have to be considered because they can put the body under stress, and thus add to the training load. If you don't take account of them, then fatigue may suddenly set in: you can't sleep normally, your limbs ache, you sweat heavily at night, you feel depressed, you can't face food – and you certainly don't want to go out training!

A typical situation might be at the height of the season with big events approaching. You are nicely into progressive overload training, and there's a domestic problem. Maybe you have to move house or your wife has left you, you're getting married or you've exams to face, your boss is giving you a hard time at work, or the taxman is writing you letters. Maybe you're travelling a long way to races, your diet is upset, or you miss your normal sleep. Suddenly it's all too much.

In these circumstances you certainly shouldn't continue to try to train normally. You need to rest, and you have to work to recover.

First of all, see your doctor to rule out any health problems, just in case. If you have a clean bill of health, then set out to regain your previous balanced situation.

Look for some good food to add to your diet. Eliminate alcohol, and cut down on tea and coffee. Increase your intake of vitamin C and B complex. Vitamin C helps to de-toxify your body; it's worth taking a daily supplement of one gram (which you can take in soluble tablet form, obtainable from any chemist). Vitamin B complex helps in several ways, especially with the nervous system; a daily dose at this time should be 50–100mg. Both these vitamins are water-soluble, and therefore cannot be any danger to you. Any excess just comes out in the urine.

Try to get as much rest and sleep as you can. Go to the cinema; read books and magazines unconnected with cycling. If you want to train, do fartlek training. Enjoy the sunshine; get a massage. All these changes and remedies will combine to help recovery.

However, prevention is better than cure, so try to avoid this situation by monitoring your body signs, particularly pulse rate. Be aware of the effect of domestic changes on your training routine, and compensate for them with a period of easier training when the domestic load is unusually high, even if it is only on your nerves.

You can also get a feeling of staleness when there is little or no variety in your training. Beware of setting yourself a routine covering the same roads day after day. You might think it helps to compare your performances; but you are also becoming dependent on it, like a drug, and if you are forced away from this regular route you can become convinced that your training is valueless. One extra reason for keeping a training diary is that you can review it with your coach or soigneur and identify possible reasons why you have overtrained or become stale.

Although we indicated earlier that the resting pulse rate is a good guide to your progress, it doesn't always give a full indication. Your resting rate may be normal, but sometimes you just don't feel right. So here again you have to take a holistic view: look at your whole organism, and ask yourself, 'Am I right?' That doesn't mean that you have to do a lot of deep thinking. The problem with bike-riders, and in fact most athletes, is that they under-think: they don't seem to give enough consideration to what they are doing. It's just a matter of following a schedule.

Sometimes a rider can do the opposite, and spend too much time on self-analysis, agonising about what is usually a very straightforward situation. Athletics coach Eric Brees aptly describes the situation: 'Too much analysis creates paralysis.'

Generally the British rider falls into the first category: he doesn't think enough. He would rather be given a firm schedule stating 'You must go out for X miles' – or he will blindly follow the training methods of a top European or national star rider, published in the cycling journals, which of course will have little relevance to him.

You should listen to what your body is telling you; you should consider where you are going, what your aims are, and what kind of training you need to do to achieve those aims. You may need your heavy dose of LSD training as a starter for basic fitness, but beware of living on such a diet. It's easy to overdose. Look at other training methods to develop.

For improvement you need progression in training, at a carefully measured rate. Stop progressing, and you will simply remain at a certain level. Progress too fast, and you will have to ease back to allow your body recovery time. In theory, good progressive training should produce a steady upward curve in performance; but in practice, your performance forms a series of plateaux at higher and higher levels. You improve, reach a new level of output, allow your body to adapt, then go on to a higher level again.

Self-doubt is dangerous

Everybody will venture an opinion on training routines. Some people insist that their method is correct for everyone, while others observe quite rightly that they get results in another way. The result is that you are surrounded with a lot of advice about training.

It isn't surprising, therefore, if you give way to doubt, and start to ask yourself whether you are really doing enough. The doubt gnaws away at you; you start to think you should be doing more and more; and you stop heeding your body signs.

Clearly the amount of pressure you impose on yourself will eventually depend on your goals, and the harder you decide to train, the more you risk overtraining.

So once again, watch out for a general feeling of weariness: every day your legs are tired even when you're lying down; you can't work up any enthusiasm; you tend to drop off at odd times, then wake up in the middle of the night; you aren't thinking as clearly; your speech tends to slur; you haven't enough energy to carry on your normal daily tasks.

These are the classic signs of overtraining, but they don't show themselves all at once. You won't suddenly wake up one day to all these symptoms and then realise you've overtrained. It all happens gradually, and this is why it is so important to be aware of what your body is telling you all the time. Noting your pulse and weight in your training diary is not enough. Write down how you feel, every day, and then you can check back easily if you suspect that you are suffering from overtraining.

After tough events at the height of the season, heed your body signs for the danger signals of overtraining.

No bike-rider ever goes through a season without having some kind of health problem. Even minor health problems can develop into major ones if they aren't handled properly, and a blind faith that they will simply go away is not enough to ensure that it will happen.

One of the advantages of being fit is that you can often shake off certain ailments quicker than the unfit person. On the other hand the very demands of cycle racing and training can put you in line for more trouble than the average person. So let's examine some of the more common problems that bike-riders face, and consider how best to minimise their adverse effect on your progress.

Colds

You have to face them every year, but 'taking them up the road and riding them out of your system' is not the answer. That is an old idea and one which physiologists and doctors now regard as potentially dangerous.

Colds come in various forms. If neglected they can be very dangerous, but you can normally deal with them yourself if you act promptly at their onset. Take normal common-sense precautions: stay indoors in the warm, keep your body temperature up, take plenty of fluids and get plenty of rest.

The recommended way to speed the cold on its way would be to take two water-soluble aspirins every four hours during the day (up to a maximum of eight tablets a day), alternating with one gram of vitamin C in effervescent tablet form every four hours. So the two-hourly dosage would be alternately aspirin, vitamin, aspirin, vitamin, and so on. Halfway through the first day you will be feeling worse, but as the day continues you will feel much, much better. It is sometimes possible, using this method, to clear a cold up within a day.

Colds should only last a day or two anyway. People who say they've had a cold for a week should see their doctor for appropriate medication.

Bronchitis

Cyclists are vulnerable to bronchitis because they train and race in all kinds of conditions.

It is vital that you should not train while you have bronchitis. Stay indoors, take vitamin C, and use inhalations. These inhalations should be of Olbas Oil (a blend of natural oils which has many healthy uses for the athlete) or of Bengue's Balsam. Have a bowl of very hot water, with either a few drops of Olbas Oil or about an inch of Bengue's Balsam dissolved into it. Put a towel over your head and gently inhale the vapours. Do this several times per day and the bronchitis will gradually clear up.

If you go training with bronchitis you will only make it worse. Make no mistake, bronchitis can be a slow killer. We know of a case where a rider neglected a cold; it turned to bronchitis, and he never really shook it off. Over a period of years he lost weight, his health deteriorated, and eventually he died.

If you definitely have bronchitis,

Racing in cold and wet conditions makes cyclists vulnerable to chest complaints.

which is characterised by difficult and painful breathing, you must call in the help of your doctor.

Coughs and sore throats

These are often caused by having to gulp down a lot of cold air – a typical situation in racing or training. The consequent drying-out of the back of the throat starts an irritation and a cough.

If you are bringing up highly-coloured mucus, then you should go to the doctor; but if the product of your cough is white, you can usually take one of the expectorants. If you are coughing without producing mucus, then you should take one of the cough suppressants which are freely available. Bear in mind that many cough mixtures contain substances which you are forbidden to race with, and which will certainly be detected in a dope test.

Sore throats can be treated by gargling with salt water or water with two drops of Olbas Oil. If you have a slight temperature, the aspirin/vitamin C procedure will often clear it up; but if it persists for more than a week, refer to your doctor.

An alternative treatment to ease a sore throat or an unproductive cough is a mixture of glycerin, lemon and honey. This can be bought from any chemist, or made yourself, with a teaspoon each of honey and glycerin, plus the juice of a lemon, mixed with some water. Sip it slowly. It's quite a pleasant way of easing your problem.

Saddle soreness

This is best avoided by riding in shorts with good-quality chamois, which are regularly washed and the chamois subsequently lubricated with products such as Jecovitol, Cramer's Skin Lube, Cetavlex or lanolin. This decreases friction between the saddle, the shorts and the sensitive perineum – the area between the legs which bears all the body weight on the saddle.

If you do get saddle soreness, all you can do is rest for a while; apply some Cetavlex or other soothing cream, and wait until the tenderness and redness has disappeared before stepping up your mileage again.

However, if you have to ride with saddle soreness – maybe at a big event or the final stage of a long race – then you can have recourse to a product called Nupercainal, which is antiseptic and somewhat anaesthetic too. It can also be used over broken skin.

Saddle boils are a nasty problem, but again they can usually be avoided by careful washing of the perineal area with good-quality soap or Phisoderm.

If you do get a boil, you must treat it very carefully to avoid the spread of infection. Don't ride the bike at all (it will in any case be too painful). Wash it several times a day with warm water to speed up the healing process, and to soften the skin so as to help drainage when it eventually ruptures. Under no circumstances allow anyone except a doctor to squeeze the boil.

If it doesn't clear up, refer to a doctor anyway. He will either lance it or give antibiotics. Never let an unqualified person treat a boil other than by helping to bathe the area with warm water.

Cramp

There are several causes of cramp: mineral deficiencies, calling on your muscles to do more than they are accustomed to, hyperventilating, or awkward positioning of the limbs. Bike-riders usually get cramp because their muscles are being called upon to perform beyond their level of training.

Cramp is caused when the muscles go into sustained contraction: they shorten as the effort is made, and then stay at their shortest, giving a sharp pain that cannot be ignored. It can last a few seconds or a few minutes, depending on how unlucky you are.

There are ways that you can ease cramp, however. A typical problem area with cyclists is the large muscle mass of the calf. You should press fairly firmly with your thumb into the thickest part of the muscle and hold for a count of ten. As you put the pressure on, you will feel the cramp gradually easing. This is the best remedy. Another method is to put the affected muscle into the stretch position, which is temporarily quite painful because it works against the contracting action of the cramp. A third solution is to use a proprietary cold spray.

If you know that the cramp is due to loss of mineral salts through excess sweating, then you should remedy the cause of the cramp by taking one of the electrolyte-replacement drinks on the market. These are intended to replace the various body salts in a balanced way. On no account take salt tablets, since normal sodium chloride (table salt) is present in so many supermarket foods that you are highly unlikely to be deficient. The most likely deficiencies among body salts are of potassium and magnesium, and it is very easy to keep these in balance by drinking fruit juices. No tablets are needed.

Hyperventilating

This is not a regular problem in cycle sport, but it can happen among riders of a high standard, so it is worthwhile being able to recognise and solve this problem.

It happens when you over-breathe, resulting in a loss of carbon dioxide into the atmosphere. This means the body gases are out of kilter. You breathe very rapidly, and have a feeling you are about to suffocate. There are touches of cramp and general body pains.

Hyperventilating usually happens at the completion of a very fast race, with high-intensity racing over the final stages. You are gulping in air but breathing out more carbon dioxide than is normal. And carbon dioxide is needed to signal the brain to breathe in again.

The sight of a rider apparently fighting to get his breath is enough to send you rushing for the oxygen bottle, but it is the opposite which is required. The simple and very efficient solution is to get the rider to breathe into and out of a paper bag or similar receptacle, so that he starts to inhale his own exhaled carbon dioxide, and the balance is thus re-established. Keep reassuring the rider that he is doing the right thing.

Antibiotics

These aren't a problem in themselves, but they are a regular treatment for all kinds of infections and need to be properly understood. First of all, resist the temptation to stop taking them when the symptoms of your infection have eased. It is vital that you take the complete course.

Another consideration is the possible interaction with certain supplements you might be taking for other reasons. If you are taking any iron or mineral supplements, stop them during your antibiotics

course. Once it is completed, resume them, preferably as part of a general multi-vitamin plus iron supplementation course.

Antibiotics also interact with milk, butter and cheese, which reduces their absorption into the system. The oxytetracycline type of antibiotic is particularly liable to this. Best to cut down on these dairy products during the course.

Antibiotics have the unwanted effect of killing off some of the body's natural beneficial bacteria as well as the harmful ones, which allows body toxins to build up. So it's a good idea to increase your intake of vitamin C during the course (but not dosing at the same time of day as the antibiotics). To replace your natural bacteria, eat natural live yoghurt after the course.

One other adverse effect of antibiotic treatment is that your skin becomes temporarily more liable to irritation, and more sensitive to the sun; so the risk of sunburn is greater, especially at high altitudes.

Recovery from illness and injury

If you have had an enforced lay-off due to illness, then your progress back to full training must be gradual. Take a multi-vitamin supplement, keep to a good diet, avoid spicy foods, keep off alcohol, and build up progressively until you feel ready to train at maximum.

If you crash, and are left with any kind of injury that is causing you great pain, then you must see a doctor – because great pain is your body's warning signal.

If you have an illness or injury that persists longer than a couple of weeks, even though you think you are on the road to recovery, it's

better to see a doctor for reassurance and any necessary treatment.

Back pain

Pain in the area of the lower back is not uncommon among cyclists. Cyclists can have prolapsed discs and similar problems which would, of course, need medical diagnosis. But many of the nagging pains are simply caused by tension in the low back muscles. The basic racing position on the bicycle, coupled with the way we use our backs under effort, produces tension in the hip and low back region. It usually starts with an ache in the lumbar region and in the deep part of the buttock. This ache is in muscles used for driving round the pedals, which are especially stressed when big gears are used. It can suddenly be brought on by indecision when riding in a group. A rider attacks, you wonder whether to jump after him, and you start to make the effort while your muscles are tense. When the effort is over, sometimes the muscles stay contracted, which puts pressure on the various nerve sources around the muscles – and you get backache.

Usually you can ease this by stretching: lie on your back; bring your knees up into your chest and your head down to meet your knees. This exercise can be incorporated into your daily stretching routine as a guard against backache. If the condition doesn't ease with stretching, then you must go to a qualified medical practitioner or an osteopath for treatment. If any back pain is intense, then you must seek medical advice.

Knee problems

Cyclists can get tendon, ligament or cartilage problems like anyone else, and any prolonged condition should be looked at by a doctor. But many knee problems are caused by the thigh muscles working excessively, especially on cold, wet or windy days. At the end of a hard ride in such conditions, when the quadriceps muscles have been continually contracting and have got gradually tighter, you tend to get minor muscle pulls at the muscle insertions around the knee area. If you use ice massage and quadriceps stretches, the condition often eases in a couple of days. If it persists, then seek qualified help.

Ice massage is a simple and effective technique. You put two or three domestic ice cubes into a polythene bag and stroke it slowly

Cold and wet races predispose you to soft-tissue injuries.

Frenchman Bernard Hinault was at the peak of his career when he had to cut back his cycling abruptly because of knee trouble.

over the knee area. Keep the bag moving until the ice has dissolved. Then do the stretching exercises. Do this twice a day. Ice massage stimulates the deep circulation and slightly anaesthetises the area so that gentle stretching can be performed without pain.

Crash damage

Any injury following an accident which involves severe pain, possible fractures or injuries to joints or ligaments should be seen by a hospital or family doctor. Until this happens, the standard procedure is **RICE:**

R is for **rest:** this prevents further damage.

I is for **ice:** the application of an ice pack or ice massage will reduce bleeding from damaged blood vessels by making them contract. This will reduce the possibility of bruising. On no account apply heat to an injury for at least 48 hours.

C is for **compression:** this is usually in the form of a pressure bandage to control swelling. This needs to be removed before you go to bed.

E is for **elevation:** if an injured limb is elevated above heart level, the excess fluid will gradually drain away, and the associated swelling will go down.

If your muscles are sore but not sharply painful, the soreness is best eased out with a gentle ride on slow gears.

Injury treatment chart

Condition	First aid	Follow-up	Recovery time
Abrasion	Clean well with soap and water or antiseptic, taking care to remove all dirt. Apply a sterile dressing.	Watch for infection and change dressings. Expose to air so that it dries up as soon as possible.	1–7 days
Blister	Clean the area, and apply a cool compress to ease inflammation. Carry out a sterile drainage and apply a dressing.	Watch for infection.	1–7 days
Bruising	RICE for 24–48 hours.	Mild bruises should have recovered. Moderate bruises: apply a light massage above the injury, and possibly some local heat. Severe bruises: refer for medical attention.	A few days 1–4 weeks
Bursitis	Rest, and apply ice.	After 48 hours apply hot and cold contrast packs. You may need to refer for medical attention.	2–6 weeks
Cramp	Place the muscle in stretch position, and apply pressure to the belly of the muscle.	Gentle massage.	Almost immediate
Sprain (ligaments)	RICE for 24–48 hours.	If mild, after 48 hours apply heat or hot and cold contrast packs. If severe, you should refer for medical attention.	2–6 weeks
Strain (muscle)	RICE for 24–48 hours.	Treat as for sprains.	1–4 weeks
Tendinitis	RICE for 24 hours.	Apply an ice massage. If severe, refer for medical attention.	2–6 weeks

If there is pain which can be traced to a small area, you have probably torn some muscle fibres. Follow the RICE code, then after 48 hours you can apply heat which will stimulate the healing process. Heat applied before this period will only serve to increase bleeding and hence bruising.

When there is no more pain with the muscle at rest, try a short ride on low gears. If this gives no pain, gradually build up training again to a normal routine.

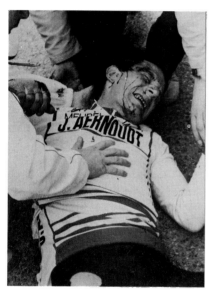

Any crash injuries need to be checked over by medical personnel.

Massage and embrocations

In a stage race, massage is essential to help get your muscles back to normal in time for the next stage.

During training, massage is not all that important – unless the training effort has been so hard that your muscles have remained tight, and some corrective massage is needed if the programme is to be continued the following day. In the main, however, stretching exercises will get most people quickly back on the road again without incurring the expense of visits to a masseur.

There are advantages to regular massage, but there is the consequent danger of becoming dependent on it. If you are used to regular massage, and you go away to race where you are without your normal treatment, then you can become psychologically down because of the lack of it.

If you are going to a masseur, make sure that he or she is trained, and is recognised by one of the associations. There are a lot of 'rubbers' about who are enthusiastic but untrained, and can just as easily rub the form out of your legs. Experienced masseurs can usually identify a rider who is used to going to a 'rubber', because he is usually insistent on a deep, hard technique. It isn't the fierceness of the rub that should count, but whether the masseur's technique is easing the aches.

Before and after

The techniques of pre-race and post-race massage are radically different. Before a race you need a stimulating technique – brisk and of short duration. The muscles should be enlivened and not sedated. Bear this in mind even when you are putting on your own embrocations, since a similar technique is necessary. Slow, purposeful movements are used after the race. If used before competition, they will have a negative effect, and the rider will need to ride himself in during the opening miles instead of being ready when the flag drops.

Self-massage

This is well worth the effort. You can gradually perfect your technique to become self-reliant, and because you are on the receiving end of your own massage efforts you can best judge their effect.

You cannot use the same techniques as a trained masseur: firstly because you will not have the knowledge; secondly because you cannot put yourself in the right position to treat your muscles as can a masseur, who is free to approach from any angle.

For simple self-massage, start in a sitting position with your back supported. Make yourself comfortable, and bend your knees. In this position massage your calf, moving from the ankle up to the back of the knee in a steady, stroking movement, moulding your hands to the contours of the muscles. Gentle but firm pressure is needed, and rhythmical movements. From the back of the knee continue the treatment to the hamstrings at the back of the thigh and the quadriceps at the front. Then you can give the thigh deeper treatment by clasping it each side and moving up the thigh, rolling the entire muscle mass around the thigh-bone, forward and back. Finish with the stroking movement again.

The effects of the rain and cobbles of the Paris-Roubaix classic can be eased by the proper use of embrocation.

Embrocations and massage lubricants

One of the best and most easily obtained lubricants for self-massage is baby oil. This is designed for sensitive skin and is therefore highly unlikely to produce any adverse reaction. Just use enough to lubricate, and to eliminate painful friction from the palm of the hand. Don't use so much that your hands can't keep a grip.

Some embrocations can also be used as massage lubricants. If it is a wet and hard day, it is probably worth using one of the milder massage creams such as Radian, Sports Rub or Musclor 1. You need just a gentle warmth. The warmer rubefacients are not designed to be used for massage, since they require only surface application. Massage them in and you risk an unpleasant burning sensation.

Creams are fine for dry weather, provided that the strength matches the temperature; but for wet weather you need a petroleum-based embrocation such as Cramer

Atomic Balm, which will not wash off in the rain. In cold weather, use plenty of embrocation around the knees, and on the calves and thighs. Also, don't be afraid to use a medium embrocation on the lower back if it is cold and wet. The very hot embrocations such as Deep Heat, Cramer Red Hot, Musclor 3 or Algipan must be used very sparingly and never on hot days. They can be applied around the knee area and over tendons.

Some embrocations come off more easily than others. The creamier ones come off in the shower, but the petroleum-based ones need to be removed with a cloth dipped in cologne or spirit. Sometimes even after removal they leave a very hot sensation, which can be countered by rubbing a cut lemon over the area.

Drugs and dope

At some time during your racing career you are likely to come up against drugs or 'dope'. There is no doubt that dope-taking has been rife in cycling, particularly in Belgium and France, but an energetic programme of dope-testing at all levels has done much to bring the problem under control.

'Dope' is any kind of preparation which could improve your sporting performance, albeit temporarily. Drugs which come under this category are listed by national federations and international governing bodies. If you are found to have used them, then you are liable to heavy penalties, fines and/or suspension.

Taking drugs to improve your performance unfairly is morally wrong. It hits against the very idea of sport, in which one man pits his strength and skill against another. To make use of a chemist to boost your own strength unfairly seems to negate the whole idea. Those riders who have used drugs have sought artificial help to succeed, and in doing so have admitted to themselves that they cannot succeed without this artificial help. So even to contemplate the use of drugs is halfway to admitting failure.

In the 'bad old days' there were a few well-meaning or unscrupulous coaches, soigneurs or managers who would administer drugs under the guise of tonics or vitamins. When challenged, they would fall back on the argument that 'everybody uses them'. Before dope-testing became widespread, this may have had more than a grain of truth. Now it is not so.

Thanks to the research which has been pioneered at London's Chelsea College under Professor Becket, dope-testing has come on apace over the past decade. In the beginning, the dope-takers would move from one drug group to another as the chemists perfected methods of detecting it. But gradually, testing methods have become so sophisticated that there is very little that cannot easily be identified from a rider's urine sample, quantified, and a fair assessment made of when the drug was taken.

It is highly recommended that you do not take any kind of preparation during the racing season unless you are positive that it contains no forbidden substance. Many proprietary cold remedies and cough mixtures can contain proscribed substances which will show a positive result, even though in such preparations they could give you no physical lift.

If you are in the slightest doubt about anything you are thinking of taking, get qualified information. The national federation will handle such queries for international riders, and often your local pharmacist will be helpful if you explain the circumstances.

Bear in mind that some brand names hide their contents, and some drugs have several different names – so be doubly careful! Here are the main groups of drugs which are on the proscribed list:

Stimulants of the central nervous system

These are, according to Chelsea, the most effective aids to performance. They can improve your performance, but are frequently addictive. They are very easy to detect and will therefore get you nowhere if you use them when there is a dope test – which can happen at random nowadays, not just in major events. Riders who have used them indiscriminately in the past have disappeared from the racing scene to have a drug rehabilitation cure!

Anabolics

These are substances which, if taken over a period of time, will allow you to improve because they allow you to train harder. Once again these are detectable; and whereas in the past their use was 'safe' because they could be used to good effect before the actual race, simply for improving the quality of training: even that loophole has now been closed, since testing procedures can now detect their past use.

Side effects of anabolic steroids include cancer of the liver, and hormonal changes which in turn have adversely affected the sexual capacity. They should be taken only under medical supervision, and no doctor would countenance their use as an aid to sporting performance.

Cortico-related drugs

Cortisone and similar drugs have been claimed to aid performance. They have side-effects which are frightening, for by taking cortisone you limit your body's ability to produce the substance naturally, as it does when it needs to fight inflammation. Hence your entire health is endangered. There are cases of well-known riders who have had to retire from the cycling scene because of minor infections and inflammations which their body could no longer combat.

We should distinguish here between the administration of cortisone by mouth – which is proscribed – and the admitted use of cortisone to combat injury, in the form of injections. Cortisone injections have the effect of reducing unwanted swelling in the case of inflammatory situations such as tendinitis. When first used, these injections appeared to be miraculous, especially in the treatment of joint disease; but later the side-effects became clear – that the joints were drying out and tendons even snapping. They have a place in sports medicine, but a limited one. One or two shots of cortisone in the right place can have the desired effect, but two is usually the limit if you are to avoid side-effects.

Ephedrine

This is a drug which improves the breathing – a bronchial dilator. It is widely used for colds in a variety of medicines, and works well with impaired breathing. Its only application in cycling would be to enable a rider to make the best use of his lungs when this is vital, such as in a kilometre time trial or a pursuit. Ephedrine is easily detected and of little advantage to the fit rider.

Caffeine

This is on the proscribed list but it is of dubious value. Although caffeine is present in tea and coffee, even a large amount may not be regarded as a positive result.

It is interesting that you can give yourself a small and permitted 'lift' by abstaining from tea, coffee and cocoa on the lead-up to a big race, then drinking some on the morning of the event and, if you wish, putting some in your feeding bottle. Cold lemon tea is in fact very refreshing. Caffeine tablets taken in large doses very often cause nausea during effort.

Dope-testing procedures

The incidence of dope-testing at cycle races is on the increase. It is a sad reflection on sport generally that dope-testing has become necessary to detect or deter the cheaters; but at least it is a protection for those who do not seek to gain unfair advantage over their rivals.

If you are racing at national or international level, you will one day be dope-tested; and it is therefore worth knowing the procedure beforehand so that you are not unduly worried by it.

When you are called to the dope control or medical control, you might well think 'Why me?' – unless of course you know that dope tests are regularly taken, both on riders who perform well on the day concerned, and on riders randomly selected. Although the number varies from race to race, it is normal to test the winner and the first few placed riders on the day, plus the overall leader in a stage race and a number of randoms.

You may be told to report to the control by a race official (and you will have to sign that you have been notified); or possibly the race rules will put the onus on you to check whether you have been chosen (usually the chosen riders' race numbers are listed on a board at the finish or by the showers). Find out the system for any race you ride, and remember the onus is on you to report. If you fail to report, then you will be treated as if you had given a positive dope test.

Normally you have about an hour to report to the control. At the control you will have to sign a form, and will be given two sample bottles (which you may change for others if you wish) and a receptacle in which to urinate. An official is detailed to actually see the urine pass into the receptacle (because some riders have tried to evade the test by using concealed flasks of 'clean' urine).

Your urine sample will be divided into the two bottles, which should be sealed in your presence. You will be asked to sign that this has been done correctly. If you see any possibility of error or confusion, it is up to you to object on the spot – or for your manager, if present, to do so on your behalf.

If, because of dehydration, nerves or any other reason, you are unable to produce a urine sample, you will be allowed to take fluids to help you. You may also be allowed to leave the control room by permission of the doctor (and usually accompanied by an official) if you feel a break will allow you to relax and then produce a sample on your return to the dope control.

One sample is sent for analysis, the other held in safe keeping should there be a positive result. In that case the second sample may be submitted to another testing laboratory of your choice and, if you require, it may be tested in your presence. Nowadays the systems are foolproof if operated according to regulations – but let's hope you never give a positive test!

Positive and negative reactions

As the world's knowledge of exercise physiology develops, and new training techniques are evolved, so the levels of competition are rising – and with them the stress factors connected with racing.

Competition tensions are really fear reactions, to which you will take one of two avenues of action. You can either act positively – the 'fight' reaction, or act negatively – the 'flight' reaction. Nature has provided this choice right from the start. The caveman confronted with a mammoth could decide to fight it or to turn and run.

If you choose the positive fight reaction, that doesn't actually involve you in aggression. It simply means that you direct yourself towards the task in hand. You determine to do a good ride.

Others, in similar circumstances, might act negatively, being overpowered by the situation and the possibility of losing. They tend to withdraw, worry about their image, and start to think about trouble with their gears; they remind themselves about the strength of the opposition, and how much money and back-up their rivals have. The result is that they will do bad rides.

Reactions are hard to predict: some riders are inspired by tackling a new, higher level of competition; others, often illogically, are demoralised by the prospect. You usually find that those who crack up in these situations are those who are highly excitable and easy to get out training – who train hard and do well in lesser races, but 'go over the top' in high-level competition.

Sometimes the better rides are done by riders who are not so evidently motivated – who need to be kicked into training. This type of rider finds his motivation in the environment, and derives new strength from the challenge – the thought of a gold medal, fame and fortune.

The wrong words

Some years back, when Alf Engers was conditioning himself to go for the 25-mile record, he would deliberately avoid people before the start, so that he could psych himself up for the ride, and so that he could concentrate his thoughts on that rather than be irritated by some chance stupid remark passed by a spectator or well-wisher.

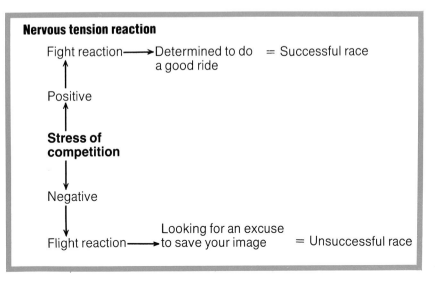

Nervous tension reaction

Fight reaction ——→ Determined to do   = Successful race
                        a good ride

↑

Positive

↑

Stress of competition

↓

Negative

↓

Flight reaction ——→ Looking for an excuse
                        to save your image   = Unsuccessful race

An example of this kind of thing occurred at the world team time trial championships at Goodwood in 1982. Before the start the rain came down, and in the closing minutes before the 'off', one of the riders' helpers remarked, 'It's going to be dangerous out there today. Have you seen how slippery the bends are?' That's not the kind of thing that will inspire a rider!

Sometimes parents or relations can send you 'over the top' by having great expectations of you, often just in order to bathe in your reflected glory. This added tension can be enough to ruin your motivation.

Before a big time trial, top riders concentrate to 'psych' themselves up. Frenchman Bernard Hinault (above) and Irishman Stephen Roche (below) collect their thoughts before the 1982 Grand Prix des Nations.

Identify yourself

So you can see it's important to find out what kind of a person you are. Are you motivated by the situation, or will you run away from it? Do you feel tense, nervous and sick, or are you happy, relaxed and ready to go? Try to analyse your rides, either at the time or afterwards, relating your feelings beforehand to the actual performance achieved.

Sports psychology is a study in itself, but to the average bike rider it is just a matter of getting the best out of yourself. You have to overcome any negative reactions and set your sights on success.

You shouldn't be afraid of losing, provided you have done your best. It is usually the desperate fear of losing that makes people take the flight reaction. But if you have trained and prepared correctly, if you know that you are fit and able to 'do a ride', if you have assessed the competition realistically and by winning the event you can achieve

a goal, you can take a positive reaction to the race.

Provided that your training, diet, and sleep is right, and that your bike is in tip-top shape, there is every reason to suppose, given the right opportunity, that you can fight your way through.

Sometimes, having started the race, you puncture. The flight reaction would be to retire, accepting the excuse, telling yourself that you would have won but for the puncture. The fight reaction would be to aim for a quick wheel-change, fight to get back to the bunch, and immediately look for the group up the road and go after it.

Various occurrences in races can have far-reaching effects. There was one rider who had the talent of never making a wrong move in finishing sprints – getting the right wheel, finding the gaps, unleashing his effort at the right time. On one occasion he was doing this in the Milk Race, on a long run-in, when a rider moved over unexpectedly, took his front wheel away, and he fell. The physical injuries weren't great, but the psychological ones took longer to heal. A little later in the race the same thing happened again. As a result it took that rider a considerable time to regain his confidence and rediscover his natural sprinting talent.

It took the rider longer than necessary to recover his previous level of performance because he never realised why it had deteriorated in the first place. Hence the need for self-analysis – and possibly the comments of your coach – in honestly assessing your reactions to stress situations.

Once you have identified a situation which produces a negative reaction, then you must set about reversing the attitude. It cannot be done at a stroke, but a determination to be more positive each time will eventually bring success. In the case of our discouraged sprinter, it would have meant making a few more manoeuvres to get up through the bunch every time there was a sprint, until the day when he would find himself once more in the ideal winning position.

Psychological warfare

At some time or another you will become a target for psychological sporting warfare, or 'gamesmanship', as it is commonly known.

The best defence – if you do not wish to stoop to such tactics yourself – is to recognise these ploys for what they are. Be prepared for such tactics, and the very fact of recognising them will minimise their effect.

The apparently innocent remark can, to the wrong sort of person, become an insidious termite, eating away at the foundations of his confidence and self-respect.

In the changing rooms, for example, a remark might be made about your appearance. 'Haven't you been well recently? You don't look as fit as usual', it goes – innocent enough and easy to deny outwardly. Inwardly you begin to wonder, especially if you are already on edge for any other reason.

Your bike might also come into the conversation. One crafty Liverpudlian rider would squint at a rival's bike and say it looked 'a bit out of track'. The target of the remark would frequently then find himself asking his friends' opinions about his bike before the race, when he should have been concentrating on getting himself ready.

If you are the kind of rider who likes to sit quietly before a race start, especially a time trial, then the gamesman might come over and engage you in meaningless and concentration-breaking chatter. Or even worse, he might send one of his associates to do the same job. If you are that sort of rider, then make sure you are tucked away somewhere out of reach of this tactic.

Feeding stations during the race provide other opportunities. One rider might start the race with pockets crammed with food, and then blast straight through the feeding station, launching an attack. This leaves other riders with the awkward choice of either reacting to the attack and missing their food, or taking their food and having to chase afterwards. It pays always to have some food and drink in reserve for just this situation. When you approach a feeding station you should be prepared for problems to occur. Unscrupulous riders will watch for their rivals shaping to take a musette of food from their roadside helpers, and then ride in between rider and helper to stop the musette being handed up. If you were the rider and you were counting on getting that food, this tactic would be a big psychological blow.

Another tactic used during the critical closing stages of a race is for a rider to produce a small flask from his back pocket and take a swig from it. The impression would be that the flask contained some wonder preparation which would give the rider concerned a last-minute boost. In practice, the flask need contain only water!

On the track, delaying tactics can be psychologically damaging, especially in events involving only two riders or teams, such as individual sprints or pursuits. The Italians are past masters at timing this to advantage, letting their opponents come to the start-line and then keeping them waiting on some minor pretext, mechanical or otherwise, just long enough for concentration to start ebbing away. The counter-move, if you are kept waiting unduly, is to wait for your opponent to start to make for the start-line, then set off on a warm-up lap so that *he* is the one kept waiting. Alternatively, especially in team pursuits, if you are expecting delaying tactics then do just the opposite. Let your team get to the mark very smartly, thus calling attention to any delay so that your opponents are hurried along by the starting judges.

The defence against psychological attacks is to have unshakable confidence in yourself and your ability. You need to have analysed yourself to get a realistic picture of the way you have trained, your successes, your strengths, the back-up behind you. Check the state of readiness of your body, your mind and your bike; and if you are confident that everything is right in all three departments, then you are pretty secure against psychological attack.

Mental training

This self-assurance is only of value, however, if your ambition is based on your true level of ability. You must set yourself progressive goals during the season. Set your sights on attaining these goals by imagining yourself on a winning ride; go over the race in your mind, seeing yourself in a good position, making the right moves on climbs and corners, taking descents well, positioning yourself correctly in the sprint. The more detailed your mental image of the race, the more effective is this method of psyching yourself up. Your conception of the 'right' move goes into your subconscious, so that the move becomes instinctive when the situation occurs. All your energy is then available for turning the pedals.

Just as physical training needs to be progressive, so this mental training must develop. You will get better at it the more you practise it.

Analyse your performances

If you do not reach the level to which you aspire, then try some self-analysis. After each race, look at it realistically to see what went wrong. No rose-coloured glasses, please – no excuses – just a sensible dissection of what actually happened. But don't be excessively hard on yourself either. If you can honestly say that you have raced competitively, then count that as a good point. Not every lost race need be seen as a disaster. Many of them may be near-successes, because perhaps only one small element of your race riding was not quite up to scratch.

Subsequently develop your strengths still further, and work on the areas where you acknowledge that you have not reached the required level. If you continue this process, then your confidence must grow. The knowledge that you are physically prepared, together with your positive mental attitude, will give you the self-confidence to turn a good performance into a victory.

In a race, virtually everyone is trying hard, even the riders who are far off the back of the bunch. The winner is the rider who has the just confidence, the inner arrogance, that he is going to cross the line first. For confidence based on a realistic self-analysis is the greatest key to sporting success.

11 *Final words*

It may have taken you a long time to read this book, but we hope that what we have taught you will have saved you much more time spent learning the hard way.

Levels of coaching vary world-wide from the rudimentary to the highly advanced, but one thing is common to every nation: the bike-rider's thirst for knowledge. Not every rider will aspire to international stardom. Fewer still will actually reach their goal. But there is no rider who cannot benefit from good advice, whatever his level.

There is no easy way to the top of cycle racing. It is bound to be hard along the way. But it isn't necessary to do everything the hard way, and there is certainly no need to learn about training and technique through personal experience alone. Trial and error takes up too much valuable training time.

Determination to succeed goes a long way. But you must also have a commitment to proper training as well as a willingness to work hard. You need to understand how your body works, and how the various training methods affect you, before you can appreciate the value of what you are doing.

We have brought together our experience and written it down in this book, in the firm expectation that there will always be riders who want to know how to succeed. If what we have said helps bring riders to international stardom, then we shall all be delighted. But if on the way it helps a reader to beat a personal best, or to win a club championship he had not previously dreamed of, then that is just as much a justification of what we have written.

Further reading

Burke, E. J., *Toward an Understanding of Human Performance* (Mouvement Publications) USA, 1977.

Dick, F. W., *Sports Training Principles* (Lepus Books) Wakefield, 1980.

Dick, F. W., Paish, W. and Johnson, C., *Strength training for athletics* (British Amateur Athletics Board) Leatherhead, 1978.

Lear, J., *KTG Weight Training* (EP Publishing Ltd) Wakefield, 1983.

Morgan, R. E. and Adamson, G. T., *Circuit training* (Bell & Sons Ltd) London, 1961.

Orlick, T., *In pursuit of excellence* (Human Kinetics, Inc.) USA, 1982.

Haycock, C.E., *Sports Medicine for the Athletic Female* (Van Nostrand Reinhold Co. Ltd) Wokingham, 1980.

Mirkin, G. and Hoffman, M., *Sports Medicine Book* (Little, Brown and Co.) USA, 1981.

Ricci, G. and Venerando, A. (Editors), *Nutrition, Dietetics and Sport* (Edizioni Minerva Medica) Italy, 1975.

Appendices

Gear table

Sprocket (Number of teeth) → / Chain wheel (Number of teeth) ↓	11	12	13	14	15	16	17	18	19	20	21	22	23	24	25	26	27	28	29	30	31	32	33	34	35
42	103.0	94.5	87.2	81.0	75.6	70.9	66.7	63.0	59.7	56.7	54.0	51.5	49.3	47.3	45.4	43.6	42.0	40.5	39.1	37.8	36.5	35.4	34.4	33.4	29.
43	105.5	96.7	89.3	82.9	77.4	72.5	68.3	64.5	61.0	58.1	55.2	52.7	50.4	48.3	46.4	44.6	43.0	41.4	40.0	38.7	37.4	36.3	35.2	34.1	30.
44	108.0	99.0	91.4	84.9	79.2	74.3	69.9	66.0	62.5	59.4	56.6	54.0	51.6	49.5	47.5	45.7	44.0	42.4	41.0	39.6	38.3	37.1	36.0	34.9	31.
45	110.4	101.2	93.4	86.8	81.0	75.9	71.5	67.5	64.4	60.7	57.8	55.2	52.8	50.6	48.6	46.7	45.0	43.4	41.9	40.5	39.1	38.0	36.8	35.7	32
46	112.9	103.5	95.5	88.7	82.8	77.6	73.1	69.0	65.4	62.1	59.1	56.5	54.0	51.8	49.7	47.8	46.0	44.4	42.8	41.4	40.0	38.8	37.6	36.5	32.
47	115.3	105.7	97.6	90.6	84.6	79.3	74.6	70.5	66.8	63.4	60.4	57.6	55.2	52.9	50.8	48.8	47.0	45.3	43.7	42.3	40.8	39.7	38.5	37.3	33
48	117.8	108.0	99.7	92.6	86.4	81.0	76.2	72.0	68.2	64.8	61.7	58.9	56.3	54.0	51.8	49.9	48.0	46.3	44.7	43.2	41.8	40.5	39.3	38.1	34.
49	120.2	110.2	101.8	94.5	88.2	82.7	77.8	73.5	69.6	66.2	63.0	60.1	57.5	55.1	52.9	50.9	49.0	47.2	45.6	44.1	42.6	41.3	40.1	38.9	34
50	122.7	112.5	103.9	96.4	90.0	84.4	79.4	75.0	71.1	67.5	64.3	61.4	58.7	56.3	54.0	51.9	50.0	48.2	46.5	45.0	43.5	42.2	40.9	39.7	35
51	125.1	114.7	105.9	98.3	91.8	86.0	81.0	76.5	72.4	68.5	65.5	62.5	59.8	57.3	55.1	53.0	51.0	49.1	47.5	45.9	44.4	43.0	41.7	40.5	36
52	127.6	117.0	108.0	100.3	93.6	87.8	82.6	78.0	73.9	70.2	66.9	63.8	61.0	58.5	56.2	54.0	52.0	50.1	48.4	46.8	45.3	43.9	42.5	41.3	36
53	130.0	119.3	110.0	102.2	95.4	89.4	84.1	79.5	75.3	71.5	68.1	65.0	62.2	59.6	57.2	55.0	53.0	51.1	49.4	47.7	46.2	44.7	43.4	42.1	37
54	132.5	121.5	112.1	104.1	97.2	91.1	85.7	81.0	76.7	72.9	69.4	66.2	63.4	60.7	58.3	56.1	54.0	52.0	50.3	48.6	47.0	45.6	44.2	42.9	38
55	135.0	123.7	114.2	106.0	99.0	92.8	87.3	82.5	78.1	74.5	70.7	67.5	64.5	61.8	59.4	57.1	55.0	53.0	51.2	49.5	47.9	46.4	45.0	43.7	39
56	137.4	126.0	116.3	108.0	100.8	94.5	88.9	84.0	79.5	75.6	72.0	68.7	65.7	63.0	60.4	58.1	56.0	54.0	52.1	50.4	48.7	47.3	45.8	44.5	39
57	139.9	128.2	118.3	109.9	102.6	96.1	90.5	85.5	81.0	76.9	73.3	69.9	66.9	64.1	61.6	59.2	57.0	54.9	53.1	51.3	49.6	48.1	46.6	45.3	40
58	142.3	130.5	120.4	111.9	104.4	97.6	92.1	87.0	82.4	78.3	74.6	71.2	68.0	65.3	62.7	60.2	58.0	55.9	54.0	52.2	50.5	48.9	47.5	46.1	41
59	144.8	132.7	122.5	113.8	106.2	99.6	93.7	88.5	83.6	79.6	75.8	72.4	69.3	66.3	63.7	61.2	59.0	56.9	54.9	53.1	51.3	49.8	48.3	46.9	41
60	147.2	135.0	124.6	115.7	108.0	101.2	95.3	90.0	85.3	81.0	77.1	73.6	70.4	67.5	64.8	62.3	60.0	57.8	55.8	54.0	52.2	50.6	49.1	47.6	42

Health history details your doctor may require

Name: _____   Date of birth: _____

Address: _____   Name and address of G.P.: _____   Occupation: _____

                                                                            Tel. home: _____

                                                                            Tel. business: _____

Record of illness (give details):   Details

☐ Diabetes	☐ Hepatitis	
☐ Rheumatic fever	☐ Anaemia	
☐ Bladder or kidney infections	☐ Polio	
☐ Glandular fever	☐ Asthma	
☐ Bone or joint disease	☐ Allergy/hay fever	

Please answer 'yes' or 'no' to the following –

Have you had any injury to the –

Have you ever –
- ☐ been knocked out?
- ☐ passed out?
- ☐ been concussed?

- ☐ neck?
- ☐ spine?
- ☐ bones?
- ☐ joints?

☐ Do you have any metal or plastic plates, pins or joints fitted?

List operations:

_____

List all medication or diet supplements you are currently taking:

_____

List any drugs or medication to which you have an allergic reaction:

_____

List vaccinations, inoculations etc. you have had (giving dates):

_____

Have you ever been advised not to participate in any sport?

Index

F

fartlek training 80
fast-twitch muscle fibres 78
fatigue 135–138
fats 121, 129–130
feeding *see* nutrition
female cyclists *see* women
   cyclists
finishing sprint 45–47
fitness 77, 82–85, *see also*
   training
flexibility *see* stretching exercises
following a wheel *see*
   wheel-following
food *see* nutrition
footwear 24, 52, 57, 75, 101, 102
frames 16–17, 51, 56, 59
further reading 153

G

'gamesmanship' 151–152
Gaul, Charly 28
gear-changing 31
gear table 154
gearing 18–20, 51–52, 57, 60, 101
girls *see* women cyclists
Giro d'Italia 40, 49
Gisiger, Daniel 21
gloves *see* mitts
glucose 121, 124, 129
glycogen 121, 124, 129
Grand Prix des Nations 150
growth and repair of body tissues
   121

H

Hallam, Ian 68, 119
handicap racing 65
handlebar position 21–22, 52, 57
handlebars 20, 57, 60
Harris, Reg 59
Hayton, Dudley 26
headgear 24, 52, 60, 61, 75, 101
health 82, 102, 131–148
   older cyclists 111
   women 112–113, 115
   see also nutrition

health history details 155
heart, how to train the 78, 84–85
Herety, John 11, 29, 68–69, 131,
   133
Het Volk, Belgium 37
high altitudes 134
high-intensity training 72–73,
   81–82, 85
hill climbing *see* climbing
   technique
hills *see also* descending
Hinault, Bernard 7, 17, 22, 49, 53,
   86, 142, 150
Hoban, Barry 28
home exercises 94–98
'honking' 28–29
hot weather 106, 108, 135
hour-a-day fitness programme
   116–119
how training works 82–85
hygiene 76, 131–132
hyperventilating 140–141

I

ice massage 142, 143
illnesses 138–141, 155
injuries 141–144, 155
interval training 70–71, 80

J

jerseys 23–24, 75, 101
jet-lag 133–134
Jones, Graham 133
Jones, Mandy 114, 115
Jones, Steve 133

K

Kapitanov, Viktor 10
Kashirin, Yuri 10
keirin 68
Kelloggs criterium 14
Kelly, Sean 9, 22, 47
kilometre time trials 65–66, 70
knee problems 142
Knetemann, Gerrie 37
Kopylov, Sergei 78
Koupovets, Viktor 60

L

lactic acid 79
Lemond, Greg 33, 35, 105
Liege–Bastogne–
   Liege 40, 45
lone breaks 39–40
long-interval training 80
long steady distance training 79,
   82–85
looking after yourself *see* health
LSD *see* long steady distance
   training

M

Madison racing 68, 73
Maertens, Freddy 86
making a break *see* breakaways
manager, team 49
Martin, Marianne 106
massage 127, 144–146
mechanic, team 49
medical examinations 82, 111,
   131, 143, 144, 155
medium-interval training 80
menstruation 112–113
mental approach *see* psychology
mental training 152
Merckx, Eddy 16, 39
Milk Race 9, 10, 14, 39, 40, 49,
   127, 129, 150
Millar, Robert 43, 74
mitts 24, 61, 75
monitoring progress 85–86, 102
Moore, Willi 68
Moser, Francesco 7, 19, 25
motivation 149–150
motor-paced racing 68
mountain conditions 134
multi-gym 90–92
muscle injuries 143
muscle pain 79
muscle types 78

N

Nakano, Koichi 59, 63, 64
'natural', the 8–9